Changing the Grade

A Step-by-Step
Guide to Grading
for Student Growth

JONATHAN CORNUE

Alexandria, Virginia USA

1703 N. Beauregard St. • Alexandria, VA 22311-1714 USA
Phone: 800-933-2723 or 703-578-9600 • Fax: 703-575-5400
Website: www.ascd.org • E-mail: member@ascd.org
Author guidelines: www.ascd.org/write

Deborah S. Delisle, *Executive Director;* Stefani Roth, *Publisher;* Genny Ostertag, *Director, Content Acquisitions;* Julie Houtz, *Director, Book Editing & Production;* Joy Scott Ressler, *Editor;* Chanel James, *Graphic Designer;* Mike Kalyan, *Director, Production Services;* Andrea Hoffman, *Production Specialist;* Keith Demmons, *Production Designer.*

All material from the Common Core State Standards for Mathematics © 2010 by the National Governors Association Center for Best Practices and Council of Chief State School Officers. All rights reserved.

Benjabi Bobcat logo designed by Don Cornue.

PAPERBACK ISBN: 978-1-4166-2539-1   ASCD product #118029   n1/18
PDF E-BOOK ISBN: 978-1-4166-2541-4; see Books in Print for other formats.

Quantity discounts are available: e-mail programteam@ascd.org or call 800-933-2723, ext. 5773, or 703-575-5773. For desk copies, go to www.ascd.org/deskcopy.

Library of Congress Cataloging-in-Publication Data

Names: Cornue, Jonathan, author.
Title: Changing the grade: a step-by-step guide to grading for student growth/Jonathan Cornue.
Description: Alexandria, VA: ASCD, [2018] | Includes bibliographical references and index.
Identifiers: LCCN 2017045553 (print) | LCCN 2017056439 (ebook) | ISBN 9781416625414 (PDF) | ISBN 9781416625391 (pbk.)
Subjects: LCSH: Grading and marking (Students)–United States. | Academic achievement–United States–Evaluation
Classification: LCC LB3051 (ebook) | LCC LB3051 .C6384 2018 (print) | DDC 371.27/20973–dc23
LC record available at https://lccn.loc.gov/2017045553

26 25 24 23 22 21 20 19 18   1 2 3 4 5 6 7 8 9 10 11 12

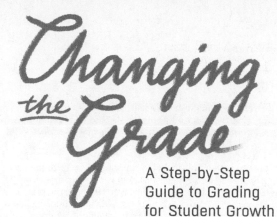

Changing the Grade

A Step-by-Step
Guide to Grading
for Student Growth

Acknowledgments

I would like to thank the staff of the Madison-Oneida Board of Cooperative Educational Services (MO BOCES) in Verona, New York, for all that they have contributed to this book. I truly love my job, and the people with whom I work are a testament to the importance of a positive culture that promotes risk-taking and basks in good humor!

In particular, I would like to thank David Arntsen, for taking me into the MO BOCES fold so many years ago and guiding me to become a more thoughtful educator; Jim Seybert, the epitome of the Renaissance man, for helping me learn to see the bigger picture while staying focused on the kids; Karen Pinkham, for initially bringing me into staff development and providing me with so many opportunities to grow and experiment; Maria Papa, my "work-wife" and "paper-keeper," for a decade's worth of fruitful conversations and wonderful comradery; Kristin Capotosto, Melissa Middleton, Ann Pangburn, and Jody Popple, for putting up with my endless questions, for their willingness to share their great wealth of knowledge, and for making our office such a joy to enter; Tracy Pulverenti and Liz Miller, for keeping me as organized and together as it is possible to make me; Ed Rinaldo—the best boss a guy could hope for!—whose willingness to let us "go ahead and give it a shot" is the reason this book was written; and Jacklin Starks, Patricia Vacca, and Scott Budelmann—the district superintendent and assistant superintendents, respectively, at the MO BOCES—whose leadership, and the *grace* with which they approach their positions, truly sets the tone for our region.

Thank you to the educators in our region (and beyond), who have answered my questions, experimented with my ideas, and freely shared their thoughts, concerns, and successes with me. I continue to grow as an educator through your generosity.

I am indebted to ASCD staff members Genny Ostertag, who took my "Oh, what the heck, I'll try writing a book" submission and encouraged me to keep at it until it was something of value, and Joy Scott Ressler, whose sense of humor and attention to detail has made the editing process a pleasure. I'd also like to thank Lorraine Coffey for her work on the book.

Thank you also to my family: my parents for their unending support and encouragement (thanks for the Benjabi Bobcats logo, Dad), and my brilliant brothers and their brilliant spouses for their love and support. David and Milena—remember that this is your fault!

And, of course, I need to thank The Boy and The Bride. Xavier, thank you for letting me experiment on you—whether you knew it was happening or not! You are a spectacular young man! Cindi, thank you for being my critical eye, my sounding board, and my best friend—and for all of the "home-life overtime" that you put in to get me to the point where I had the foundational knowledge to write this book. *Always.*

Introduction: Why Should We Change Scoring and Grading Structures?

My Boy is a pretty darn good kid. He is currently in 10th grade. He is an *A* student, a soccer player, a Boy Scout, self-motivated, personable. And he still listens to his parents (mostly). He is the type of kid who comes home from school, grabs a snack, watches a little YouTube, and then says, "OK, I'm going to do my homework now." He has always been that way. He is also the catalyst that sparked my interest in scoring and grading structures.

When Xave was in elementary school, he came home with an 80 on a social studies assignment. The assignment had five multiple-choice questions and an extended response question that he had to answer in one paragraph. All of the multiple-choice questions were answered correctly, and the comment "Good job," was written next to the essay. I turned to The Bride, who is also an educator, and said, "I'm confused. Why is this an 80?" Mind you, I wasn't worried about it. An 80 on an elementary-level social studies assignment isn't going to keep him out of Harvard. But it made me curious.

Over the years, my job as a staff development specialist for the Madison-Oneida Board of Cooperative Educational Services in Central New York, serving a nine-district region, has allowed me to develop trusting relationships with a number of teachers. So I made a copy of the completed assignment with Xavier's name, comment, and grade removed. Then I went to another teacher of the same grade, in the same district, but at a different building. I asked her to score the paper. She gave it two possible grades—an 88 *or* a 91.

I said again, "I'm confused. Why might the grade be one or the other?"

The teacher responded, "I don't know this child. If he or she typically struggles, then this shows good effort, so I would bump the grade up a bit."

"Huh," I thought. "Good effort can increase a social studies grade. Well that makes sense. I did the same thing when I taught high school English. We're educators. We like kids. We want them to feel good about themselves. What difference does adding a few points make? It might encourage that child to continue to work hard."

So then I took the paper to *another* elementary teacher of the same grade level in a different district. She gave the assignment a 4.

And again, I said, "I'm confused. How do I translate that as a parent?"

The teacher explained that in her district, a 99–100 was a 4. A 97–98 was a 3.9, and so on. Each tenth of a point on a four-point scale was correlated to a couple of points on a 100-point scale.

Essentially, the grade on my son's paper ranged from an 80 to a 100, depending on the classroom in which it was evaluated. Take a moment and think about your school's grading system. Might a similar experiment show the same discrepancies? What if you took it to a neighboring district? How comfortable are you with the accuracy of your scores? What does it even mean to be "accurate"? Which of the three teachers "correctly" scored Xavier's paper?

Look, we are all different. These three teachers are excellent, which is why I felt comfortable asking them to look at the paper. But the reality is that we come to our positions with different histories and different backgrounds. My youngest brother, for example, was much better prepared to be a teacher than I was—he got Piaget, Bloom, Hunter, Marzano, Wong, Tomlinson, and Wormeli and I studied Piaget, Bloom, and a little Hunter. Unless we are taught otherwise, most of us at least begin by teaching the way we were taught, and scoring the way we were scored. And that's what was happening with Xavier's paper. The teachers scored it based on their own expectations, backgrounds, and experiences.

Again, I wasn't worried about My Boy in the big scheme of things, but I started to think about the effect of a 20-point swing. What if it occurred in 11th grade instead of in elementary school? What if it was a test instead of a homework assignment? What if the 20 points were the difference between a 60 and an 80 instead of an 80 and a 100? What effect might that have on employment opportunities, on college opportunities, on scholarship and grant opportunities?

I began to dig into scoring and grading practices. I read a lot. I went to conferences. I chatted with the experts. I asked questions of teachers and principals and district leaders from across the country. There is a great deal of research on this topic, and I think that most educators, at least intuitively, recognize that we need to change our models. So why haven't we done so?

AN ARGUMENT FOR CHANGE

Honestly, I believe the lack of movement on this issue comes down to two legitimate concerns. First, we don't know how to make the change, and, second, we are afraid that making the change will negatively affect our students because employers and colleges won't know how to appropriately *interpret* a new grading system.

To address these issues, what we really need is a concrete structure, a way to plan for the change. We need to ask *quality* questions: Why should we change? What, specifically, needs to be changed? What actions must be taken in order to facilitate the changes? We need to ensure that all of the stakeholders—teachers, counselors, administrators, parents, board members, the community, colleges, and students—understand that this is not "This Year's New Thing," an educational movement that is interesting for now, but soon to be replaced by "Next Year's New Thing." We need to demonstrate that this process is intentional, research-based, student-focused, and permanent.

This change isn't easy. I know, because I am currently rolling it out to a few of the buildings in our region. The model laid out in this text cannot be accomplished in a few weeks, or even a few months. But the end result will be a systemic and systematic shift to a quality structure that is far less subjective than many of the models more commonly found in schools.

If we are to accurately and equitably evaluate student learning, if we truly want a model that provides quality information not just to Xavier's "educator-parents," but to *all* parents, if we want an evaluation system that fosters *learning*—it is a change that needs to occur.

READING THIS TEXT

I once saw a descriptor of change that looked something like the picture in Figure I.1, which is relevant to this text.

Figure I.1 Change is Hard

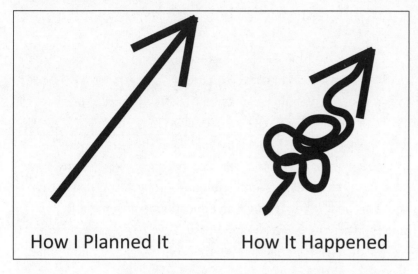

How I Planned It   How It Happened

As you are reading this book, which is relatively linear—and outlines 30 specific steps to move toward a significant grading system change—keep in mind that no plan is perfect. The human element plays a role in making a change as significant as this. I imagine that you will find yourself, after the first read-through, jumping back and forth a bit. Just keep in mind leadership expert Robin Sharma's quote: "Change is hard at first, messy in the middle, and gorgeous in the end" (Sharma, 2010). You will get to the gorgeous!

1

What We Know About Grading

To initiate a building- or districtwide shift in scoring and grading practices, we need to first ensure that we can clearly identify what needs to be changed, as well as explain why those changes need to occur. As you read through the ideas in this chapter, begin to ask yourself, "Why do we grade? What is the purpose of a report card grade? How do these ideas apply to my school and district? Who else should be thinking about this? What is my first step in initiating *interest* in this topic?"

This chapter provides an overview of the changes we should make in the grading model. Subsequent chapters will dig into the "how" of the change and will address some of the "yeah, buts" (such as, "Yeah, but will the colleges accept these changes?").

SOMETHING OUT OF ONE HUNDRED

Melanie is a fantastic high school English teacher in my area, so to follow up on the mini-experiment I conducted with my son's social studies assignment (as described in the Introduction), I asked her for an assignment she gives to her 12th grade students, along with a student response that was in the "85-to-95-percentile range." I distributed the on-demand writing assignment and student response, sans identifying information, to approximately two dozen 12th grade English teachers, along with the link to an online survey. Additionally, I asked them to share the assignment and survey with other 12th grade English teachers that they knew. The instructions on the survey were pretty straightforward: Score this assignment as you would score an assignment in your classroom. I provided numerous models for scoring: 100-point scale, four-point scale, four-point scale with halves, four-point scale with tenths, five-point scale, letter scales both with and without "plus" and "minus" options. You get the idea. I even provided an "other" option in case someone used a model I didn't list.

The results were telling. Of the 23 respondents, 16 used the 100-point scale. The highest grade was a 95. The lowest was a 70. In other words, the score had little to do with the child's understanding of the material and ability to clearly convey that understanding. Where this child went to school and the teacher to whom she was randomly assigned would determine whether she was struggling to get out of high school or exploring grants and scholarships for college.

For good measure, I did the same with an 11th grade social studies assignment and a 12th grade physics assignment. I had fewer respondents (14 and 6, respectively), but the results were similar. In each case, there was a 20-point gap in the scores when the 100-point grading system was used.

Of course, I was not the first person to perform this kind of exploration. Starch and Elliott did the same thing with 142 English teachers and returned similar results—in 1912. They later performed the same study with 138 geometry teachers and came back with results that ranged from the mid-20s to the mid-90s, all based on the same student paper (Starch & Elliott, 1913). More recently, Hunter M. Brimi (2011) duplicated Starch and Elliott's experiment with 73 English teachers. The high score on the shared assignment was a 96; the low score was a 50.

Apparently the disparities in our scoring and grading models have not changed much over the past 100 years.

So what is our first step in appropriately changing the grading system? Remove the wildly unreliable 100-point grading model.

FOUR POINTS—THAT'S IT

If we eliminate the 100-point grading system, how do we track students' grades?

To answer that question, we have to first answer this one: *Why should we give grades to students?* Ask that question of 10 educators, and you will probably receive 10 different responses, such as:

- To let the child know how she is doing.
- To let me know how he is doing.
- To let the parents know how their children are doing.
- To let employers know how well the child did.
- To let colleges know how well the child did.
- To guide my instruction.
- To guide the interactions next year's teacher will have with the child.
- Because the school told me to do so.
- That's the way we have always done it.
- I never really thought about it. We just *do*.

What you will probably *not* hear is: "To rank the child against other children in the school." There is really no purpose to such an action. Ranking does not better inform parents, children, or colleges as to what a student has learned. It doesn't guide your instruction. At best, it boosts an ego. At worst, it destroys one. There is no research supporting the idea that giving children a failing grade encourages them to "work harder" (whatever that means).

Besides, ranking children is not our purpose. Ideally, our education system is a bit more socialist in structure; every child should have an equal opportunity to succeed and should never be measured on a curve. Our goal is to help all students learn to the best of their abilities, right? If such is the case, then we really only need to ask these questions:

1. Has the child attained the level of mastery that the standards set for this topic?
2. If yes, is she where I want her to be, or has she surpassed the expectations set by the standards?
3. If no, does she need a little support, or a lot of support, to get there?

These three questions become the foundation for a four-point grading system:

1. Surpasses expectations of the standards = *4*
2. Meets expectations of the standards = *3*
3. Needs additional support to meet expectations of the standards = *2*
4. Needs a great deal of additional support to meet expectations of the standards = *1*

Four points. That's it.

You will notice that there are no decimals in this system. Robert Marzano (2010) indicates that using half points or thirds of a point might be okay, but I'm not a big fan of even that little drift back toward 100 points. Half points give us eight possible grades. Thirds give us 12 points. Can you consistently tell me the difference between a 2.3 and a 2.6? What would that look like in a standard that indicates a child should be able to "Determine the meaning of words and phrases as they are used in a text, distinguishing literal from nonliteral language" (CCSS.ELA-LITERACY.RL.3.4)?

Many researchers lean toward a four-point system for this reason (Guskey & Bailey, 2010; Jung, 2009; Marzano, 2010). A few large organizations (e.g., PARCC (Partnership for Assessment of Readiness for College and Careers), AP (advanced placement)) use a five-point system for assessments, but I am not in favor of it for everyday grading. It is too easy to drift to "middle ground" (a 3 in this case) when the scale is based on an odd number. I would rather we commit to our decisions.

"MILKING" THE STANDARDS

You may have noticed that earlier in this chapter I connected student scores to a standard, not to an assignment. That's because standards matter.

In my own surveys, the scores given by those teachers who used the four- and five-point scales were at least contiguous, although this was not necessarily true of those who used plus and minus letter-grade models or halves or tenths on the four-point model. But even changing to a four-point system is not enough.

Another issue that arises in scoring is that we don't always agree about *what* we are grading. I remember being asked by a student during my third year of teaching, "Mr. C, why did I get a 78 on this paper?" I went through the motions of pointing out things that could have been changed and improved, but what I was really thinking was, "Because I've been doing this for a few years, kid, and that's what a 78 looks like."

And that didn't sit well with me, even then. I knew there was something missing, but I had no idea what that something was. Later that year I was introduced to rubrics, which made my scoring a bit more accurate, but even then, I was simply making up the criterion categories based on instinct and educated guesses.

That was in the early days of standards in New York State, and we were just beginning to use them as general guides. Today, standards are firmly entrenched in education across the country. Some states are using the Common Core State Standards, others have individual state standards. National standards have been developed by a number of organizations for music, art, carpentry, and languages other than English. The guidelines for *what* to teach are out there. We simply need to connect them to the rubrics we use for our assignments, projects, tests, and grades.

Communication Through Standards

Let's take a look at a Next Generation Science Standard (NGSS) from the Middle School grade band. NGSS has a complicated and multifaceted structure involving Performance Expectations built from Disciplinary Core Ideas, Science and Engineering Practices, and Crosscutting Concepts, but we can still use it to develop a rubric that addresses the knowledge and skills that the students need to internalize. In Figure 1.1, you will notice that the material from the standard is placed both on the left and in the Level 3 column. The descriptions for scores of 1, 2, and 4 are then linked to that standard.

Tying student scores to individual standards is good for students. It provides them with specific goals and helps them understand their areas of strength and their areas that need additional support.

It is also helpful for the following year's teacher who, when looking at the grades that "Martin" received in your class, will be able to see more than just a 2 in mathematics. Instead, she'll see that "Martin" received a 3 in "value of numbers in the ones, tens, and hundreds place," a 3 in "sorting, classifying, and ordering," and a 3 in "measurement in inches, feet, and yards," but a 2 in "addition and subtraction." Imagine the value this data could have in that teacher's planning! Imagine its value for teachers who provide student support in academic intervention!

Finally, there is the significance of such reporting to the families, who for years have been befuddled by scores that read like this: Mathematics–73. When scores are connected to specific standards, caregivers have a guide to help them ask the right questions of both their children and their children's teachers.

Say vs. Do

We would like to be able to say, "I know the standards, and I teach to them." But that simply isn't good enough. We are human, and we tend to overlook things. We tend to forget. If you are like me, you have gone to the store to pick up four specific items, only to discover upon returning home that you only bought three, and

Figure 1.1 Sample of a Standards-Based Science Rubric*

	Level 1	Level 2	Level 3	Level 4
Student clearly demonstrates an understanding of the process and results of photosynthesis. (DCI—LS1.C and PS3.D)	Demonstrates an understanding that photosynthesis is necessary for most plant life, including algae and phytoplankton.	With teacher support, demonstrates an understanding of the process and results of photosynthesis.	Demonstrates an understanding of the process and results of photosynthesis.	Along with the criterion for a 3, demonstrates an understanding that energy input initiates the chemical process in photosynthesis.
Student demonstrates an understanding that within a natural system, the transfer of energy drives the motion and/or cycling of matter. (CC—Energy and Matter)	Demonstrates an understanding that energy is connected to growth in the natural world.	Demonstrates an understanding that matter transfer occurs in nature, but struggles to communicate the "how."	Demonstrates an understanding that within a natural system, the transfer of energy drives the motion and/or cycling of matter.	Along with the criterion for a 3, demonstrates an understanding of the connection between photosynthesis and chemical energy production.
Student is able to construct a scientific explanation based on reliable evidence and an understanding of the surety of natural laws. (SEP—Constructing Explanations and Designing Solutions)	Can follow specific, teacher-developed steps to construct a scientific explanation based on reliable evidence and an understanding of the surety of natural laws.	With teacher support, is able to construct a scientific explanation based on reliable evidence and an understanding of the surety of natural laws.	Able to construct a scientific explanation based on reliable evidence and an understanding of the surety of natural laws.	Along with the criterion for a 3, demonstrates an ability to revise an explanation based on new information.

*Based on Next Generation Science Standard MS-LS1-6—Construct a scientific explanation based on evidence for the role of photosynthesis in the cycling of matter and flow of energy into and out of organisms.

you're missing a gallon of milk. Why? Because you didn't write a list. Because you thought, "I'll remember it all." Because you didn't have a concrete, in-your-face reminder that *this* is what you need to do. Identifying standards and evaluating a student's ability to meet those standards on every assignment and assessment helps us to "remember the milk."

THIS AIN'T BASEBALL

In 1927, at the height of his career, Babe Ruth had a batting average of .356. In other words, he hit the ball and got on base about one out of every three times he came to the plate. People have kept statistics like this on baseball players for nearly as long as the game has been around. Batting average, on-base percentage, earned-run average—these are all models that help managers track the effectiveness of a player on the field. But finding the average does NOT help a teacher—a classroom manager—determine what a child has learned. And the tense of that verb is key. *Learned*. Not *learning*.

Why We Track Student Grades

Why do we track student grades? We want to see what a child has learned. Finding the average of a student's scores at the end of her learning process does little to help us figure out where to go next with our teaching.

Look at it another way. Imagine that you are 16 years old and about to begin the process of getting a driver's license. Someone takes you out and teaches you how to drive. You sit behind the wheel of the car and your teacher, Mom or Dad or Uncle Benny, says a little prayer and tells you to *gently* put your foot on the accelerator. You spend days or weeks or months practicing. You study for the written exam. Your little brother quizzes you from the practice book (because he is earning points so that you will be his taxi). You try parallel parking. You try it again. You learn to anticipate idiot drivers on the road. You learn that rushing a yellow light is generally not a good idea. And then, one day, you get to go take the road test.

Now imagine that the final test did NOT determine whether or not you received your license. What if, instead, you were graded against the "proficient driver standard" as you were *learning* to drive? What if the determination as to whether or not you received your driver's license was based on the *average* of your learning process? Or on how long it took you to become a proficient driver? It seems silly, but that is exactly what we are doing when we are averaging student grades.

In a workshop hosted by the Madison-Oneida Board of Cooperative Educational Services, Dr. Thomas R. Guskey, researcher, author, and professor at the University of Kentucky, pointed out another issue with averaging student learning: sometimes a passing average does not indicate proficiency. In his words, "Is a child proficient at crossing the street if they remember to look both ways 80 percent of the time?" (Guskey & Jung, 2015). Some concepts are too important to let slide with "close enough."

Case in Point: Marni

Let's look at the grades of fictional student Marni.

Marni is taking a grade 9 English class and has been struggling with the standard CCSS.ELA-LITERACY.WHST.9-10.4: *Produce clear and coherent writing in which the development, organization, and style are appropriate to task, purpose, and audience.*

Her scores are 1, 2, 2, 1, 2, 2, 3, 3, 2, 3, or a total of 21 out of 40 possible points on the 10 assignments. Marni's average score was a 2.1, but I give her the score of 2 because I don't use decimals. But is that actually what she has *learned*? If I look at the last few grades, it is obvious that over the course of her learning she has become pretty good at meeting this standard. Why would I punish her for sticking with it, practicing, and learning? I am an awesome teacher! Look at the skill I helped Marni develop! Her score should be a 3.

If this seems subjective, consider the evidence. Three out of her final four grades are 3s. Why did she receive a 2 on assignment nine? That's a good question. Robert Marzano (2010) suggests that we address outliers like this on a face-to-face basis. "Hey, Marni, things seemed to be going well here, and then you slipped a bit. What happened?" Maybe she had a soccer game the night before and rushed through the assignment. Or maybe there is a misunderstanding about organizational structure that needs to be cleared up. In either case, the teacher could spend a few minutes working with her, ensure understanding, and then change the grade from a 2 to a 3. The child earns a 3 because the child knows the material at the 3 level.

Of course, this is assuming that we know what a 3 means.

THE HALOS AND HORNS SYNDROME

Because we are human, most of us have experienced what I call the "Halos and Horns Syndrome" at one point or another in our careers. It goes something like this:

Halos: "Jayla has worked so hard on this paper. It still isn't where I want it, but I can't bring myself to give it a 2. It will crush her! Let's bump it up to a 3."

Horns: "Ah, Michelle. You have been a pain in my posterior for two straight weeks. Alright. Well, let's take a look at this paper and see if you are anywhere near my expectations."

The grading surveys I distributed to the high school English, social studies, and physics teachers contained a few extra statements to which the teachers were asked to respond. Their responses (Figure 1.2) are telling. It's nice to know that we aren't alone in these internal battles!

Now, I realize that this is not a formal study, but I think most educators would agree that these numbers are unsurprising; this is not a new conversation (Dueck, 2014; O'Connor, 2007; Reeves, 2011). Should we take a student's effort and citizenship and timeliness into account when scoring? If so, how much of an effect should it have on the final score?

It can be frustrating to worry about these noncontent-related issues. Teachers struggle with this debate all the time. We may begin to wonder if we should even care about these things. I'm an art teacher, not a boss! I'm a math teacher, not a life coach! I'm a fourth grade teacher, not the kid's father!

And then we get that little niggle in the back of our brains. Of *course* we need to worry about citizenship and effort and timeliness and fortitude and all of the other "soft skills" that we try so hard to incorporate into both our classrooms and our grading systems. After all, what we really teach, even more so than the subject matter, is the child.

Figure 1.2 Factors that Affect Teachers' Scoring*

	Never	Sometimes	Often	Always	N/A
I give points for effort on an assignment.	16%	44%	26%	7%	5%
I "find" points on an assignment if a student needs an extra grade boost.	33%	62%	2%	2%	0%
I subtract marking period points if a student is frequently absent.	84%	5%	7%	2%	2%
I (unintentionally!) grade "harder" or "easier" based on my personal moods.	53%	44%	2%	0%	0%
I (unintentionally!) grade "harder or "easier" based on a student's behavior.	65%	35%	0%	0%	0%

*Rounded to the nearest percentage point.

We want to—and should—teach these soft skills and report back to the child, her parents, and her future teachers as to how well that child has learned them. It's important. It helps the child set goals (yet another important soft skill). As Susan M. Brookhart writes, it is important that we "Give students ongoing formative feedback about these behaviors and suggestions for how to adjust them" (2017). Why, then, do we bury these skills in the grade or grades for the course? Instead, these elements of learning should be graded and reported separately.

IS THIS MISSION IMPOSSIBLE?

No. But making these changes will require some serious and focused work. And it will require that we understand a bit about the change process. Discussions of change theories are woven into subsequent chapters. Give them due diligence, as they are integral to effectively changing a grading structure.

2

Building the Foundation

MAKE THE ANNOUNCEMENT

So how do we start this process? To begin, discuss the *exploration* of the topic in faculty meetings. Let the district's board of education know about the research you will be doing. Chat about it over punch with the PTA/PTO. Bring it up in the grocery store check-out line. Take out an ad in the local newspaper. Shout it from the rooftops! Let it not be said that there is a "secret plan" or that "I didn't know." Every possible stakeholder in your community (including the students!) should know that "XYZ School District is exploring models of grading that improve learning structures and provide better information to the students, parents, and teachers."

It is important to use the word "exploring," which means that you are not yet committed, that we are not thrusting a new initiative upon the teachers, and that people still have a say in what will happen. Exploring also gives you the opportunity to invite people to help you explore. These are the people who will make up your Foundation Team.

ASSEMBLE THE FOUNDATION TEAM

The most important part of initiating this change is ensuring that everyone understands the goal. You want every stakeholder to have access to a person who can clearly convey the intent of and reasoning behind the shift to a new grading system. Some Foundation team members may serve double duty (e.g., the elementary teacher representative may also be the head of the union). The suggested team structure that follows should work for small to middling-large districts (10,000 students or fewer). For larger districts, I recommend the same team, but I also suggest that the district take steps to ensure that team members have an opportunity to clearly pass their learning and messages on to their colleagues (e.g., although there may be 12 principals in the district, there may be only 3 on the team. Is there a common time when they all gather so that information and concerns can be addressed?) For very large districts, I defer to the people who have expertise in that area. You know best how to organize your structures, but remember that rarely is a decision made by 50 people.

District-Based Foundation Team

The Foundation Team, even for the largest districts, should generally include:

- Elementary teacher
- Middle school teacher
- High school teacher
- Elementary principal
- Middle school principal

- High school principal
- Guidance counselor
- Special education coordinator
- Union representative (where appropriate)
- Superintendent (or designee with decision-making authority)

Building-Based Foundation Team

If your goal is to initiate a buildingwide as opposed to a districtwide change, the team can look similar; just ensure that all stakeholders are represented. A middle school-based Foundation Team might include:

- Grade 6 English teacher
- Grade 6 science teacher
- Grade 7 math teacher
- Grade 8 social studies teacher
- Technology teacher
- Middle school principal (or other decision maker)
- Guidance counselor
- Special education coordinator
- Union representative (where appropriate)

Of course, you may want to include others on these teams—a parent representative, an assistant superintendent, a technology coordinator, a teacher who represents the arts. And you can do that, but keep in mind that the larger a group gets, the harder it is to organize tasks, schedule times to meet, and stay on task. In all, there should be no more than a dozen people on the initial team. You can always bring in "special representatives" for select meetings if the team needs to hear from a specific interest group.

The Personality Mix

Another element to keep in mind is the personality mix. While we all love it when people agree with everything we say, such a structure may not be in the best interest of this project. That's not to say that we should look for antagonists. Rather, the focus should be on filling the team with critical thinkers who aren't afraid to speak up if they have a concern. All of the team members should also feel comfortable as "go to" people for the staff. Take volunteers, of course, but remember that most volunteers will be eager to explore a new grading model, so don't be afraid to hand-select a few representatives in order to balance the ranks. A cynic brings new ideas to the table, and a converted cynic goes a long way toward moving the masses.

The principal at one school with which I am working wisely chose a veteran teacher who never took anything at face value. Every statement I made was checked. By our second meeting, this person had done hours of research to determine the value of my suggestions and the merit of the project. Moreover, this excellent, thoughtful teacher took the time to *process* what he read and to come to his own decision based on the information he had. He still had questions. He still had concerns. But he was willing to work toward the goal of changing the grading system because he came to believe in it.

LEARN AND SHARE

I once spoke with a principal who introduced a move to a new grading model in January with the goal of implementing it in September. It worked! She got the community on board. Most of the teachers were in favor of the change, and the students learned the premise of the new grading system. Four years later, though, they were still "cleaning-up." Many of the standards found on the report card were incorrect. There was still significant discontinuity in grading practices. Grades were still the primary goal, and learning was a happy, if inconsistent, byproduct. The principal's comment? "I wish we had taken more time to set it up, but I was afraid of losing the momentum that we had generated."

The best laid plans often fail when the execution is rushed. Gathering the Foundation Team in June with the hope of making a significant change by August is simply unrealistic. Instead, plan for one full year to study, develop a vision statement, and convey the proposed shift to peers, friends, and students.

Study

The Foundation Team should take the first year to study (see the lists of texts at the end of this chapter). Certainly, you can't go wrong with Guskey, Marzano, Brookhart, or Dueck. Alfie Kohn (1994) has some great theories on grading, though they may get a bit "out there" for some people (e.g., should we even grade students?). Still, he has some fantastic ideas that should be considered. You may even decide to use the first chapter of this text as a starting point.

Whichever works you explore, be certain to include, early on, books on leading change. An oft-used idiom in our office is, "The only people who like change are wet babies." And generally speaking this is true—especially when that change feels forced upon us. Systemwide change can be even more difficult. How, then, does one move an entire school building or district? The short answer is, you don't. Instead, you provide an opportunity for the system to change.

The key elements of successful change. In order to effect a systematic and systemic shift in grading structure, the stakeholders or their representatives (in this case, the Foundation Team) need to understand some of the key elements found in successful change. They need to know how to build capacity and knowledge through the effective use of what Hargreaves and Fullan (2012) call "professional capital." Professional capital is where human capital (stuff that individuals know), social capital (stuff we can figure out together), and decisional capital (stuff I have learned through years of experience) come together.

There are a slew of "change" books on the market. Two of my favorites are *Switch: How to Change Things When Change Is Hard*, by Chip Heath and Dan Heath (2010), and *Mindset: The New Psychology of Success*, by Carol Dweck (2006). I highly recommend both for anyone interested in making a shift in grading, not because they speak to the topic itself, but because they help explain how such changes can occur.

Heath and Heath and the three parts of change. The Heath brothers write about the three parts of change: the elephant, the rider, and a well-prepared path. In short, the path is the direction in which we want to move. In this case, the path leads us to a different grading model. The rider is the logical part of the brain; we know that our grading system is antiquated, uninformative, and counter-productive to student learning. That leaves the elephant, which is the power of emotion. We know that the rider can't *really* control the elephant if it becomes panicked or if it decides that it doesn't want to move. So we need to ensure that the elephant feels safe and secure when it is asked to accomplish the task at hand. Only by marrying these two entities can we make our way down the path.

Dweck. And this is where Dweck's *Mindset* comes in. Her research led to the concept of a growth mindset and a fixed mindset. A person in a fixed mindset thinks, "I can't do this." The Boy (he's a "grade-grubber") was very upset about a five-week report from his school indicating that he had an 88 in art. "I don't know what to do!" he said. "I can't draw for scratch! It's just not one of my talents." We all have a fixed mindset about certain elements in our lives, and moving beyond that "I can't" attitude can be difficult.

By contrast, a person with a growth mindset thinks, "I can't do this...*yet.*" The growth mindset leads us into exploration, and exploration leads to change. It is easier to move ourselves into a growth mindset if we believe in the task at hand.

Combining the ideas of *Switch* and *Mindset* and applying them to changing our grading systems, then, looks like this: If we can logically demonstrate *why* we need to change, and if we provide the appropriate assurances, we can move the elephant toward a growth mindset and eventual change.

This sounds simple, right?

Of course not. There are all sorts of obstacles in our way: tradition, timing, the feeling that "if this were valuable someone else would have done it already."

Hargreaves and Fullan. To address this, consider asking the Foundation Team to read *Professional Capital* by Andy Hargreaves and Michael Fullan (2012). This text explores the use of human, social, and decisional capital to help a school grow. In truth, the Foundation Team needs to be as fluent in the concepts discussed in these books as they are in the texts related to grading models if the shift is to succeed.

Foundation Team discussion. When studying the texts, there needs to be an atmosphere of open discourse, not simply book reports at which everyone nods their heads. The Foundation Team should discuss likes and dislikes, questions and concerns, "aha!" moments and items that leave them dazed and confused. Their goal should be to become as well versed on scoring, grading, and systems change as possible.

All of the study should lead the Foundation Team to three realizations:

1. We *need to* change our grading system because it does not accurately reflect or properly support student learning.
2. We *can* change.
3. We *are* informed experts on this topic.

Ground rules. To truly build the team into a purposeful, functioning group, consider laying out a few ground rules at the beginning of the sessions. I highly recommend that any such group be introduced to the "Two Ways of Talking" model from Adaptive Schools (Garmston & Wellman, 1999), or a similar model. Just as important is the need to establish the overall role of the team. If the Foundation Team is advisory, but the principal or superintendent will make all of the final decisions, then full consensus is preferable but not necessary. If the Foundation Team is making the decisions, let them know that up-front. Many schools already have models in place for such discussions; just be certain that all of the participants are aware of their roles and the expectations.

Develop a Vision Statement

Early on in the study phase of this project, ask the Foundation Team to develop a vision statement. Although this term is sure to cause eye-rolling in at least half of the team, a vision statement is *critical* to the success of the project.

Rules of the vision statement. The vision statement, at this point, should follow a few basic rules:

1. *Keep it brief.* No more than three sentences.
2. *Keep it flexible.* Ensure that everyone knows the vision statement will change as they progress in their exploration and study.
3. *Keep it focused.* The topic at hand is making the grading structure more effective, and the vision statement should reflect that.
4. *Start with the "why."* The word "why" is the key to moving an organization forward.

In an inspiring TEDx Puget Sound talk, Simon Sinek says, "People don't buy what you do, they buy why you do it." He speaks to the need for people to believe before they buy into a product or an idea. I like to use this video (https://youtube/u4ZoJKF_VuA) at my first meeting with teams interested in changing their grading systems.

To that end, the Foundation Team needs to begin with that vision statement, and the vision statement needs to begin with another Sinek quote: "We believe…." The "we" is very important here. It means that the team is taking ownership of the ideas that follow. *This* is what members of the Foundation Team believe about the purpose of grading and scoring.

So how do you develop your vision statement? Toward the end of the Foundation Team's first meeting, ask everyone to jot down their answer to this question: "Ideally, *why* SHOULD we provide grades?" After a few moments, share those reasons and gather them on chart paper or a projected screen (I prefer the latter so that it can be easily changed). Then ask team members to turn those ideas into one to three sentences, beginning the first one with the words "We believe…".

CONVEYANCE

At the end of the meeting, it is important to encourage team members to share their discussions with their peers, friends, students (where appropriate), and any other interested parties. Discussion helps us solidify new learning in our brains and brainstorm new ideas. Another goal of these discussions is to begin to get a feel for where the community is on this topic. It is okay for a Foundation Team member to say, "I'm not sure that I buy into this, *yet*, but I figure it is worth exploring."

ACTION STEPS

Step 1

Build a library.

Following are suggested texts on grading:

- Brookhart, S. M. (2017). *How to use grading to improve learning.* Alexandria, VA: ASCD.
- Dueck, M. (2014). *Grading smarter, not harder: Assessment strategies that motivate kids and help them learn.* Alexandria, VA: ASCD.
- Guskey, T. R. (2009). *Practical solutions for serious problems in standards-based grading.* Thousand Oaks, CA: Corwin.
- Guskey, T. R., & Bailey, J. M. (2010). *Developing standards-based report cards.* Thousand Oaks, CA: Corwin.
- Marzano, R. J. (2010). *Formative assessment & standards-based grading.* Bloomington, IN: Marzano Research Laboratory.
- O'Connor, K. (2011). *A repair kit for grading: 15 fixes for broken grades.* Boston: Pearson.

- Reeves, D. B. (2011). *Elements of grading: A guide to effective practice.* Bloomington, IN: Solution Tree.
- Wormeli, R. (2006). *Fair isn't always equal: Assessing & grading in the differentiated classroom.* Portland, ME: Stenhouse Publishers.
- Vatterott, C. (2015). *Rethinking grading: Meaningful assessment for standards-based learning.* Alexandria, VA: ASCD.

Following are suggested works on change:

- Dweck, C. S. (2008). *Mindset: The new psychology of success.* New York: Ballantine Books.
- Hargreaves, A., & Fullan, M. (2012). *Professional capital: Transforming teaching in every school.* New York: Teachers College Press.
- Heath, C., & Heath, D. (2010). *Switch: How to change things when change is hard.* New York: Broadway Books.

Step 2

Share some of the basic ideas from Chapter 1 with the staff. Let them know that you would like to form a Foundation Team to *explore* a change in the grading system at your school in order to make it more accurate and useful.

Step 3

Identify the Foundation Team members and set the first meeting date.

Step 4

At the first Foundation Team meeting:

- Review some of your concerns about the school's current grading system.
- Ensure that the team knows its role (advisory or decision-making).
- Establish models of communication (e.g., careful listening and safe zones).
- Use Sinek's *Start with the Why* video, and then ask the team members to jot down the reasons *why* they think we should grade students. Use those ideas to lead a "We believe…" conversation.
- As a team, develop a one-to-three-sentence vision statement about grading, beginning with "We believe…." Ensure that everyone knows that this statement is subject to change.
- Present library options (articles, chapters from books, websites) on *grading*. Every member of the team should choose a piece or two to read before the next meeting. Try to ensure that no more than two people are reading the same piece in order to gain more perspectives. While reading, team members should have two questions in mind: How can we use this information to meet our vision statement? How might this information *modify* our vision statement?
- Send every team member a copy of the vision statement so they can have it on hand as they read.
- Develop three letters: one to the Board of Education, one to the staff, and one to the community. Explain that a team is "*exploring* models of grading that improve learning structures

and provide better information to the students, parents, and teachers."

- **Remind team members that they are free to talk about what they are reading with other staff and in the community in order to get feedback.**

Step 5

At the second Foundation Team meeting:

- Review the rules for discussion and the role of the team.
- Remind the team of the current vision statement.
- Ask team members to report on what they read: What seemed important to them? What questions did they have? Record these on a T-chart. Be certain that everyone shares the author and work that they read so their colleagues can find the information if they are looking for it later.
- After everyone has reported, ask the team to reconsider the vision statement in light of its collective reading. Modify it as necessary. Remind everyone that the vision statement is still the "why," and that the team will explore the "how" and the "what" at a later date.
- Ask team members to choose more readings on grading, and read them with the same focus questions in mind: How can we use this information to meet our vision statement? How might this information *modify* our vision statement?
- **Remind team members that they are free to talk about what they are reading with other staff and in the community in order to get feedback.**

Step 6

At the third Foundation Team meeting:

- Review the rules for discussion and the role of the team.
- Remind the team of the current vision statement.
- Ask team members to report on what they read: What seemed important to them? What questions did they have? Record these on a T-chart. Be certain that everyone shares the author and work that they read, so their colleagues can find the information if they are looking for it later.
- After everyone has reported, ask the team to reconsider the vision statement in light of their collective reading. Modify with the goal of identifying a "mostly finished" vision statement.
- Using the sides of the T-charts from the second and third meetings that identify the "important" changes as a guide, ask the team to develop a list of *druthers*. That is, if they had their preference, and with no consideration for the inherent difficulties in making the change, what changes would they make to the current grading system? Keep this list!
- Choose two pieces on change and assign them to small groups. For example, ask half of the team to read some of Dweck's *Mindset*, and ask the other half to read an excerpt from the Heath brothers' *Switch*. The focus questions for these works are, "How does change occur?" and "How might this information help me make the identified changes to our grading system?"
- **Remind team members that they are free to talk about what they are reading with other staff and in the community in order to get feedback.**

Step 7

At the fourth Foundation Team meeting:

- Review the rules for discussion and the role of the team.
- Remind the team of the current vision statement.
- Ask team members to report on what they read: How does change occur? What might get in the way? How could we address those challenges? This is just a brainstorming session, with the intent of "planting the seeds" of change.
- Pull out the "druthers" list. Ask team members if they are willing to commit to a plan to further explore those changes, provided they are given enough time to do it correctly.
- **Remind team members that they are free to talk about these discussions with other staff and in the community in order to get feedback.**

3

Developing the Grading Structure

WHERE TO BEGIN

When I initially began working with schools on making this shift, I believed that after four or five meetings the rest of the staff should be brought on board. Interestingly, the Foundation Teams in these buildings were dead set against this. As one teacher put it, "If we go to them without a sample of the structures that demonstrate that the changes *can* be made, we will lose half of the staff before we get started." Her colleagues agreed, and we began to work on the structures.

While this model has worked for the schools with which I am involved, you know your staff best. You may find that your building is filled with people who need to know the progress of the team early on. If such is the case, maybe you can bring the whole staff along. Again, the elements in this book are linear in format—a train, if you will, that brings you from point A to point B. That does not mean that you can't rearrange the order in which you line up the freight cars.

NOTE

The model presented in this chapter applies to elementary and middle schools. High school is covered separately in Chapter 4. Still, I recommend that you first read this chapter so as to have points of reference for Chapter 4.

NUMBERS AND NOTATIONS

As I noted in Chapter 1, I am a believer in the four-point system without the use of decimals. This system asks us to make a firm decision: Has the child met the standard or not? If little Maylee has met the standard, her work is a 3 or 4. If not, her work is a 1 or 2. If Maylee's work is well above the expectations for the standard, it is a 4. If it is well below the expectations for the standard, it is a 1. The key to this is remembering that the standard is a year-end benchmark, and that Maylee's 2 at the end of the second marking period is not necessarily indicative of a problem. Rather, it is a marker for her level of understanding.

It is important that a common language be used to describe each of these numbers for the sake of teachers, parents, and students. Therefore, one of the first tasks the Foundation Team should address is to define what "3" means, and then to use that definition as a basis for defining 1, 2, and 4. These definitions should be succinct, but the differences must be clear. The process of developing the definitions shouldn't take too long—it is really just a matter of wordsmithing. For example, for a level 2, do you prefer, "Student achieves the standard with some support" or "Student is close to achieving the standard alone"? And for most classes in grades 2–8, this is enough. Frankly, with the exception of middle school honors classes that allow students to earn high school credits, we could use peaches, apples, bananas, and coconuts to identify a student's grade, and as long as we are clear on the definitions, the system would work.

NOTE

Much of the learning in kindergarten and first grade centers on very specific, concrete, skill building (e.g., counting to 100 or knowing how to pronounce diagraphs). This often leads to a reporting system that varies from those used in other grade levels. It would be worth the time to have a conversation with these teachers to identify whether or not they should switch to a four-point model. If so, what exactly does a "2" look like in "counting to 100"? If it doesn't fit, don't force it.

REPORT CARD SAMPLER

When developing samples for the staff to use as guides, choosing a Trial Team to develop the materials is critical. A member of the Foundation Team and his or her counterparts in the classroom will set the level of expectation for the rest of the staff. Suppose you have a grade 6 common branch teacher on the Foundation Team, whose grade 6 colleagues are pretty forward-thinking and eager for the proposed change. Approach those teachers to be a part of the Trial Team subcommittee. This group has one responsibility: develop and try out the materials identified as necessary for this scoring shift so that the Foundation Team can see the elements of the change in action. The Trial Team is not committing to any permanent change, or even to a shift in the way the classroom is currently run—for now. There will be more work for this group later, but for the sake of this chapter, we are going to ask group members to define and organize the standards that they teach into elements that can be placed on the report card.

Let's take the grade 6 Common Core Math Standards (in Appendix A) as an example. If we were to record each standard and sub-standard, there would be 47 different grades on the report card for mathematics alone, not counting the 8 mathematical practices. Obviously, this is too overwhelming to be of much use. Instead, the team of teachers should work to identify groups of standards that make sense together and that are "grade-worthy."

If we were to use the Common Core State Standards math standards resource developed by Achieve the Core (http://bit.ly/ATCMath), we would discover that the statistics and probability standards, as well as one set of the number system standards, are considered "additional." This means that they are important as far as laying down a foundation for 7th grade, but not necessarily "grade-worthy." Most of the other standards for grade 6 math are a means to the deeper understanding identified by the "cluster" heading. Therefore, we might use the clusters for our report cards.

The student can:

- Understand ratio concepts and use ratio reasoning to solve problems.
- Apply and extend previous understandings of multiplication and division to divide fractions by fractions.
- Apply and extend previous understandings of numbers to the system of rational numbers.

- Apply and extend previous understandings of arithmetic to algebraic expressions.
- Reason about and solve one-variable equations and inequalities.
- Represent and analyze qualitative relationships between dependent and independent variables.
- Solve real-world and mathematical problems involving area, surface area, and volume.
- Make use of mathematical strategies (Mathematical Practices 2, 3, 4, 5, 7, and 8).

Even this, though, may be too complex for a report card. Therefore, the Trial Team may adjust the language so that it makes sense to the students and parents. We will also add a statistics and probability bullet to appease anyone who is still struggling with leaving those standards entirely off the report card. The student:

- Can understand and use ratios in real-world situations.
- Understands fraction division and why it works.
- Understands rational numbers.
- Can show how arithmetic and algebra relate.
- Understands one-variable equations and inequalities.
- Can use dependent and independent variables to solve real-world problems.
- Can apply geometric formulas to solve real-world problems.
- Has a basic understanding of statistical variability and distributions.
- Makes use of mathematical strategies (Mathematical Practices 2, 3, 4, 5, 7, and 8).

Now we have nine clear goals for the student to achieve by the end of the school year. That seems like a reasonable number of items to place on a report card, doesn't it?

Of course, it doesn't always work out this easily. Sometimes the standards cannot be simplified much. Sometimes more standards need to be included. The question to address during these discussions is this: "What standards really need to be on the report card, with the understanding that I should still teach and evaluate other standards as appropriate?" Notice that evaluation does not always mean "reported grade"!

EASING THE WORRY

One issue that arises with a standards-based report card is the concern that a standard is the goal for learning *by the end of the year*. Therefore, a student's score on a standard at the end of the second marking period may be lower than some parents would expect to see, leading to "freak-out" phone calls to counselors, principals, or board members.

This is easily addressed with a parenthetical notation built into the report cards. Teachers of a common subject, after deciding on which standards (or clusters) will be addressed on the report card, decide on the expected levels of learning for most students, most of the time, in each marking period. This number is added to the report card immediately following the student's grade for each standard. A 2 on the report card for the second marking period for the cluster "Understands rational numbers" might be a cause for concern. However, a 2(2), lets the parent know that the child is right where he or she is supposed to be.

Because this number is agreed upon by all of the teachers involved, it will be uniform across a grade level or subject area. It does not get "shifted" because one has a difficult class (yes, they exist!). Rather, it is a common *goal*.

Once the Trial Team members have placed the established standards on the mock-up report card and identified the expectation level for each marking period, their first job is completed.

AVOIDING THE FINAL AVERAGE—TWICE

At this point, there needs to be a serious conversation within the Foundation Team about the tendency we have to average grades into a single score. In a traditional 100-point model, averaging occurs at the end of the marking period. The teacher adds together all of the points that a student could have earned and divides that number into the sum of all the points the student did earn. The resulting decimal is converted to a percentage, and that becomes the child's score for the marking period. As was discussed in Chapter 1, though, this does not make sense, and we should *not* do this for each standard. We want to demonstrate what the student has learned, not the average of her or his learning.

Moreover, with a standards-based report card, there will be a temptation to average the student's scores for each standard to come up with a final subject area grade. In other words, people may want to follow a model similar to that found in Figure 3.1.

Why do this? What advantage is there to averaging the child's levels of understanding across nine different standards, especially when, in some cases, that score indicates that the child is

Figure 3.1 Simplified Standards and Scores (Inappropriately Averaged)

STANDARD	SCORE
Can understand and use ratios in real-world situations.	3 (3)*
Understands fraction division and why it works.	3 (3)
Understands rational numbers.	3 (3)
Can show how arithmetic and algebra relate.	2 (3)
Understands one-variable equations and inequalities.	2 (2)
Can use dependent and independent variables to solve real-world problems.	2 (3)
Can apply geometric formulas to solve real-world problems.	3 (2)
Has a basic understanding of statistical variability and distributions.	2 (2)
Makes use of mathematical strategies (Mathematical Practices 2, 3, 4, 5, 7, and 8).	2 (3)

3 + 3 + 3 + 2 + 2 + 2 + 3 + 2 + 2 = 22	22/9 = 2.44	2.44

*Note the parenthetical goal, as addressed in the "Easing the Worry" section of this chapter.

right where you wanted him or her to be? The score of 2.44 does not help the child, the teacher, next year's teacher, or the parents. In fact, it is just an extra and unnecessary step. Instead, we simply let the standards reflect the learning.

EVALUATING "SOFT SKILLS"

Traditional report cards generally have an option for the teacher to add a comment to the grade. For example, "The student is dedicated to her or his learning" or "The student does not complete homework in a timely manner." These are often referred to as *soft skills*, and they should not be mixed in with the grade that indicates the level of a child's understanding or skill as it relates to a particular standard.

Consider this example—

Tim has done little homework over the past five weeks in science class, yet he has completed every in-class project, taken every quiz, and nearly aced every test. He obviously understands the material. The work he *has* completed demonstrates that he has a level 4 understanding of photosynthesis. Does giving him a 3 because he doesn't do his homework actually tell him anything new? What information does a 3 on a science standard give his parents about his work habits? How does that 3 help guide the 9th grade teacher's interactions with Tim next year?

What if, instead, we made "completion of assignments" an entirely separate grade? Then we can give Tim the accurate 4 for the standard related to photosynthesis, but give him a 2 for "completion of assignments." Now we are using grading for the correct purpose—providing relatively detailed, accurate information to the stakeholders in that child's life. Of course, Tim is more the exception than the rule.

Struggling Students

Much more common in our schools is the child who struggles to achieve success. Consider your student, "Sebastian," who is a heck of an artist, a pretty good musician, and a talented mathematician, but couldn't find his home state on a map *of* his home state. Geography, historical facts, political trends, and overarching social patterns roll off his brain like water off a duck's back.

And Sebastian *tries*. He studies with his parents in the evening. He participates in class. He completes all of his homework. But when you take the support of the textbook away from him, it all starts to blend together.

Because you are a quality teacher, you provide Sebastian with graphic organizers and help him develop mnemonics and timelines to keep the information organized in his head. He gratefully tries all of your strategies, and at the end of the marking period he receives his grade for this grade 8 social studies framework-based standards:

Chronological Reasoning*: Articulate how events are related chronologically to one another in time and explain the ways in which earlier ideas and events may influence subsequent ideas and events* (EngageNY, 2015). There are three ways to report this:

1. Identifying the score for the standard ***only***: Chronological Reasoning: *2*
2. Identifying the score for the standard ***averaged with the effort***: Chronological Reasoning: *3*
3. Identifying the score for the standard and the effort ***separately***: Chronological Reasoning: *2*; Continually Strives to Learn: *4*

The first model—identifying the score for the standard only—can destroy Sebastian's hope and interest in getting better. Eric Jensen (2009) has written about the importance of instilling a sense of "hopeful effort" in relation to students who live in poverty, and we all know that this really is a key element for *any* child. The moment a child decides "I can't," well, they can't. The second model—identifying the score for the standard averaged with the effort—is simply inaccurate. Sebastian does *not* have a level 3 understanding of that standard, and so should not be given that score. The final model—identifying the score for the standard and the effort separately—is really the only logical method for accurately reporting on Sebastian's learning *and* his effort. It demonstrates "hopeful effort," and once again more accurately reports the child's learning on both the standards *and* the soft skill.

Dissecting the Whole Grade

To truly report a child's learning, then, we need to dissect the "whole grade" into multiple parts: the standards (discussed previously) and the soft skills. Which soft skills to evaluate and how they are defined may vary from school to school, and maybe even from grade level to grade level, but consider limiting identified skills to three or four overarching ideas that address multiple concepts. For example:

- *Citizenship*. Effective group member, shows kindness to peers, empathetic
- *Effort*. Meets deadlines, attends to details, perseveres
- *Attitude toward learning*. Strives to learn, grows from feedback

It is important to have a conversation about how many levels there will be on the scale by which these skills are scored. This really depends on how the team chooses to define each element —and they *must* be defined. The more specific the definitions (e.g., completing fewer than 80 percent of assignments lowers the "effort" score), the more continuity there will be across the school or district. Have a conversation about the support such scoring will provide to the student and teacher. For example, if a child receives solid "effort" scores in English and science, but not in social studies or math, teachers may look more closely at the models of instruction being used to garner that child's interest.

Also, consider using a letter code for this part of the report card in order to avoid confusion with the learning standards scores. For example:

M: Meets expectations
R: Meets expectations, with **R**eminders
OR
M: Meets expectations
R: Meets expectations, with **R**eminders
S: Struggles to meet expectations
OR
E: Exceeds expectations
M: Meets expectations
R: Meets expectations, with **R**eminders
S: Struggles to meet expectations

Product, Process, and Progress

If we put standards-based grading together with expected levels of learning at each quarter and the soft-skill evaluation model identified here, we have an evaluation system that addresses what Thomas Guskey and Lee Ann Jung (2015) refer to as "product, process, and progress," respectively. *That* is what makes up a complete report card, as demonstrated later in this chapter.

Equally important is that this model of grading is no more difficult than the model most schools currently use, and the **learning** is better recorded. Consider this: we aren't recording any more grades than we have in the past and we always mark in our books how students are doing. Now, though, instead of averaging the grades given to students, we are using our *professional judgment* (Guskey & Jung, 2015) to determine a child's score for the associated standards based on that child's end results. Instead of sorting through dozens of comments to find the right fit for each child, we have simplified the process while placing more emphasis on key soft skills by giving them a grade. Once the report card and grade book are set up (Figure 3.2), the grading process is simple.

USE OF "N/A"

Using a "not applicable" reference is perfectly acceptable. If you don't teach a concept until the third quarter, it makes no sense to grade it in quarters one and two. By the same token, if a concept is taught in only the first two quarters, and not *meaningfully* addressed in quarters three and four, an "N/A" may apply. However, if the students, for example, are taught two-digit multiplication in the first quarter, and then apply it throughout the year, it makes sense to continue evaluating their growth, so grading would continue for that standard.

Figure 3.2 Sample of the Math Section of a Report Card with Soft Skills

Milena Gose, Team 6A

Marking Period		1	2	3	4
Mathematics	**Student:**				
NS.6 Cluster A	Can understand and use ratios in real-word situations.	1(2)	1(2)	3(3)	3(3)
NS.6 Clusters B and C	Understands fraction division and why it works.	2(2)	2(2)	3(3)	3(3)
NS.6 Cluster D	Understands rational numbers.	1(1)	2(2)	3(3)	3(3)
EE.6 Cluster A	Can show how arithmetic and algebra relate.	2(2)	2(2)	3(3)	3(3)
EE.6 Cluster B	Understands one-variable equations and inequalities.	N/A	2(2)	3(3)	4(3)
EE.6 Cluster C	Can use dependent and independent variables to solve real-world problems.	N/A	2(2)	3(2)	4(3)
G.6 Cluster A	Can apply geometric formulas to solve real-world problems.	N/A	N/A	3(3)	N/A
SP.6 Clusters A and B	Has a basic understanding of statistical variability and distributions.	N/A	N/A	N/A	2(3)
MP	Makes use of mathematical strategies (Mathematical Practices 2, 3, 4, 5, 7, and 8).	2(2)	2(2)	2(3)	3(3)
Soft Skills					
Citizenship: Effective group member, shows kindness to peers, empathetic		M	M	M	M
Effort: Meets deadlines, attends to details, perseveres		M	R	M	M
Attitude Toward Learning: Strives to learn, grows from feedback		R	R	M	M

Key*	
Standards-based scores are based on **end-of-year expectations. ** Parenthetical numbers (e.g., (2)) indicate the goal for level of understanding at that point in the year. (N/A = not applicable)	4—Exceeds expected level of understanding 3—Meets expected level of understanding 2—Meets expected level of understanding, with support 1—Meets basic level of expected understanding, with support
Soft Skill scores identify the student's approach to learning and the learning environment. For example, a child may struggle with content but be very conscientious about the learning process.	E—**Exceeds** expectations M—**Meets** expectations R—Meets expectations, with **Reminders** S—**Struggles** to meet expectations

*The key should be universal and only identified once on the report card (see Appendix B).
**Standards Based on Common Core State Standards for Mathematics, Grade 6.

ACTION STEPS

(continued from Chapter 2)

Step 8

At the fifth Foundation Team meeting:

- Review the rules for discussion and the role of the team.
- Remind the team of the current vision statement and modify, if necessary.
- Provide a sample section of the report card (such as the one shown in Figure 3.2), and ask Foundation Team members to dig into it. What do they like? What do they have questions about? What do they dislike?
- Discuss each part of the report card including clustered standards and the reasons to use them; parenthetical scores and how they relate to a student's actual score, as well as the reason to have them on the report card; soft skills; and the lack of a final average.
- Decide as a team which of these parts you will keep, and which, if any, the team wishes to discard.
- Define the scoring system numbers—4, 3, 2, and 1.

- Decide whether the soft skills will be buildingwide or defined by grade. If the former, identify the soft skills that will be evaluated and the scoring system that will be used.
- Ask the team to spend some time thinking about a group that might be willing to try clustering standards before the next meeting.
- **Remind team members that they are free to talk about these discussions with other staff and in the community in order to get feedback.**

Step 9

Use the group's notes to develop a sample *blank* report card. (There is no need to include the standards or grades as this is simply a visual representation of the work done to date.)

Step 10

At the sixth Foundation Team meeting:
- Review the rules for discussion and the role of the team.
- Remind the team of the current vision statement and modify, if necessary.

NOTE

At this point, the team should be comfortable with its vision statement. If there is still a need for significant change, stop here until the concerns have been addressed.

- Share the sample report card with the Foundation Team. What do team members like? Does anything need to be changed?
- Decide on a Trial Team that will experiment with completing the report card. This could be as simple as 2nd grade teachers

or 7th grade social studies teachers or studio art teachers. This will go better if at least one member of the Foundation Team is on the Trial Team.

- Decide on the best way to approach the Trial Team and to introduce members to the changes that are being *considered* (remember, nothing is set in stone yet). Set a time frame for getting that work done.
- **Remind team members that they are free to talk about these discussions with other staff and in the community in order to get feedback.**

Step 11

Approach the Trial Team and share the Foundation Team's work to date. Get a commitment from the team members to complete the appropriate blank spaces in the sample report card.

- Set a time frame and *provide time within the school day* for the completion of the work.
- Ensure that Trial Team members understand that they have three responsibilities:
  — Develop standards-based clusters and place them on the sample report card;
  — Identify the parenthetical grades for each standard at each marking period using the definitions developed for 4, 3, 2, and 1 as a guide; and
  — Track the time it took to complete this work and any significant issues they had while working.
- Collect the completed work and associated notes.

- **Let Trial Team members know that they are free to talk about their work with other staff and in the community in order to get feedback.**

Step 12

At the seventh Foundation Team meeting, review the work done by the Trial Team.

- Review the rules for discussion and the role of the team.
- Remind the team of the vision statement.
- Identify noted issues with the process. Is the process reasonable, or do changes need to be made?
- Take note of the time needed to complete the task.

NOTE

Generally, the Trial Team is made up of willing participants. It may take other teams longer to do the same work. In the future, use the Trial Team's notes as a yardstick to plan for the work.

- **Remind team members that they are free to talk about these discussions with other staff and in the community in order to get feedback.**

4

The High School Variation

The reality of high school necessitates a change in the model described in Chapter 3. In a perfect world, colleges would recognize the shift that is being made and the value of acknowledging a level *above* "meets the standard." In a perfect world, the focus would be placed on student learning above all other considerations. In a perfect world, high school structures, which are supposed to be designed so that they meet the need of *every* student, would guide college structures, which are designed to meet the needs of only those students who choose to attend college. Unfortunately, this is not a perfect world, and in this case, it seems that the tail will continue to wag the dog.

SURVEYING COLLEGES

In 2013, I sent a survey to 476 colleges across the country asking how they would view a four-point grading system similar to the one described in this book. Of the 58 responses I received from admissions officers, 10 said that a transcript that used a traditional 100-point grading system or a traditional 4.0 grading system (with one-tenth variations) was "very important" in their decision-making process. These decision makers worked at very different types of schools: large and small, private universities and state colleges. Another 23 said that they would prefer a traditional model, but would consider other models. The final 25 indicated that the model of grading was "not important" or "not important, as long as we can figure out what the score means." Only three colleges said a nontraditional transcript (e.g., one from a home-schooled student) would have a "serious impact" on that child's admission chances.

One of the survey questions asked the following:

> A transcript lists 20 standards[1] for grade
> 12 ELA. A student receives the following:
> Level 2 on two of the standards (indicating
> "approaching grade level understanding");
> Level 3 on 14 of the standards (indicating
> "met grade level understanding"); Level 4
> on four of the standards (indicating "above
> grade level understanding"). How might
> this be interpreted?

Six of the colleges indicated that this student would be a "poor candidate" for their institution. Seven said that the student would be a "sure candidate." Another 41 responded that the student would be a "possible" candidate. About 45 percent of the responding colleges indicated that if this student received similar

---

[1] The idea of grading 20 standards for one subject may seem excessive. This is the maximum I would recommend. Not all of the standards would be evaluated every quarter (see Appendix B, Grade 4, Math, for a sample).

grades in all of her other subjects, she might be eligible for a merit-based scholarship.

Why the Variation?

There was such a variation because colleges don't just look at grades. They consider a student's entire body of work. Did the student improve over time? Did she take difficult courses? Did she make the most out of what her school had to offer?

It is also important to note that there was no discernable pattern to these responses. Some prestigious universities and tiny junior colleges indicated that they could work with a new system; and some prestigious universities and tiny junior colleges indicated that they had concerns with the system I proposed. Regarding merit-scholarships, one admissions officer wrote, "Typically the top 5–10 percent of our applicant pool receives academic merit awards, so it depends on the strength of our pool—not on your grading system." Another wrote, "I entirely reject this system."

No Hard and Fast Rule

There is no hard and fast rule for getting into college. Some colleges use SAT scores, others don't. Most consider community service (voluntary, of course). Some put more emphasis on the "core" subjects, but most consider the whole child.

The Realities of College Admission

We need to be honest here: college admissions officers receive thousands, sometimes even tens of thousands, of applications each year. In chatting with a few of these decision makers, I learned that they often spend less than four minutes per transcript. Many don't look at individual class grades unless a student is applying for a particular school of study within the college (e.g., the engineering program at a college may have specific entrance requirements in math and science). Instead, they just look at the final average. One admissions counselor told me she has a chart on her wall that allows her to easily convert four-point, five-point, seven-point, and letter grades to a 100-point scale. Asking every college admissions officer in the country to take special note when they see a transcript from "XYZ" School District, and asking them to remember that a "3" means the child is right on track to attend college, is simply not reasonable.

ADJUSTING THE MODEL

This means that at the high school level, we need to adjust the language used to describe a "4," a "3," a "2," and a "1." In high school, a "4" needs to become *the student meets the standard,* or some variation thereof, in order to keep pace with schools that give 90s to students who meet the standards.

Do I love it? No.

Is it realistic? Yes.

How, then, do we properly credit those students who are exceeding the standard? The easiest way to do this is to weight the final score for those students. By entering a "4*" for a particular standard at the end of a course, the teacher is essentially bumping up an advanced child's score. Many schools already do this for advanced placement, International Baccalaureate, and similar classes, to account for the fact that these students are challenging themselves with a more difficult level of study. Many counselors from around the country with whom I've spoken told me that their districts offer a .1 "bump" to the final average for high-end courses, so a similar bump for students who have exceeded the "meeting the standards" goal certainly has precedence.

NOTE

Adding the 4* to this grading system changes it to a five-point system, of sorts. Again, this is not my ideal, but it is a reasonable concession, given our end goals.

FINDING THE AVERAGE

Another element that needs to be addressed is the need for a final average in each course, along with an overall GPA at the end of a child's high school career. While we recognize that these are important to colleges, we also need to remember that remaining standards-based in our scoring guides student learning and teacher instruction. So how do we bring these two structures together?

Many high schools, or at least departments within the high schools, have a set pattern for determining a grade. For example, homework is worth 20 percent of a student's final grade, classroom participation is worth 10 percent, quizzes and projects are worth 50 percent, and unit exams are worth 20 percent. The idea behind this is correct, but the percentages are tied to the wrong elements. Instead of tying a student's scores to the *tools* that help us determine her or his understanding, we should tie it to the understanding itself. Therefore, when a high school team sits down to "cluster" standards, team members should also take the time to determine the worth of each cluster. Do we only spend two weeks on this concept? Maybe that is worth 5 percent of a student's grade. Is this a recursive concept that we address all year long? We should make that 14 percent of the student's grade.

And let's remember, too, that the standards we are using to evaluate student learning are year-end goals. There is no need for a final average at the end of each marking period. Rather, we should look only at the final scores for each standard to determine the grade.

The Light at the End of the Tunnel

Consider the report card sample in Figure 4.1. Imagine the change in mindset that this model presents. Daniella was obviously struggling with ELA at the beginning of the year. The "S" (Struggles to meet expectations) tells us that she did not put much effort into her learning and that she seems to have an attitude that will only continue to hold her back. If Daniella is in a "typical" grading model and receives 40s or 50s in the first marking period, and if she understands that her first, second, third, and fourth marking period grades will all be averaged together, she may decide, "I'm in too deep a hole to climb out of. And besides, I can't do this stuff."

What if, though, we help Daniella understand that we only plan to consider the demonstrations of *final* understanding? We can instead say to her, "You are struggling, but all that matters is where you are in your understanding at the end of the year. Let's keep at it!" Now we have a child who knows the light at the end

Figure 4.1 Sample of the English Section of a Report Card with Soft Skills—High School

Daniella Gotham, Grade 10

Marking Period		1	2	3	4	%	Grade
ELA	**Student can:**						
RL.9–10. Key Ideas and Details	Use text-based inferences to analyze theme and character motivations.	1(2)	2(2)	3(3)	4(4)	10	.4
RI.9–10. Key Ideas and Details	Use text-based inferences to analyze ideas in nonfiction texts. Summarize objectively.	1(2)	2(2)	2(3)	4(4)	10	.4
RL and RI.9–10. Craft and Structure	Analyze how figurative language, structure, rhetoric, and point of view impact fiction and nonfiction works.	1(2)	1(2)	2(3)	4(4)	10	.4
RL.9–10. Integration of Knowledge and Ideas	Analyze the connections between a work of fiction and other works of art and writing.	N/A	N/A	2(3)	3(4)	15	.45
RI.9–10. Integration of Knowledge and Ideas	Analyze and evaluate nonfiction works in various forms of media, assessing validity, relevance, and historical value.	1(2)	2(2)	3(3)	3(4)	5	.15
W.9–10. Text Types and Purposes	Understand the elements and uses of argumentative, explanatory, and narrative texts, and can write them accordingly.	1(2)	1(3)	2(3)	2(4)	10	.2
W.9–10. Writing Skills	Produce coherent writing with strong development, organization, planning, and revision, using technology, as appropriate.	1(2)	1(3)	2(3)	2(4)	15	.3
W.9–10. Research to Build Knowledge	Effectively research, analyze, and synthesize from multiple sources to answer a question or solve a problem. (Both fiction and nonfiction)	N/A	2(2)	4(3)	4(4)	10	.4
SL.9–10. Present Ideas and Knowledge	Present information effectively and as appropriate to given audiences and circumstances, using media strategically.	N/A	N/A	2(3)	4(4)	5	.2

Marking Period		1	2	3	4	%	Grade
ELA	Student can:						
L.9–10. Language and Vocabulary	Demonstrate the use of appropriate grammar conventions in writing and speech; continue to enhance vocabulary.	1(3)	1(3)	2(4)	3(4)	10	.3
						Final Average	3.2
Soft Skills							
Citizenship—Effective group member, shows kindness to peers, empathetic		R	M	M	M		
Effort—Meets deadlines, attends to details, perseveres		S	R	M	M		
Attitude toward Learning—Strives to learn, grows from feedback		S	R	M	M		

of the tunnel isn't an oncoming train! We begin to see growth. We acknowledge her researching skills, and yet we clearly demonstrate that although her hard work has improved her writing, she needs to keep at it. This is useful information to the student, to parents, and to *next year's teacher*!

In Figure 4.1, the second column from the right (the percent column) indicates the percentage that the grade 10 ELA team members agreed each standard is worth. The final column on the right demonstrates what Daniella earned for a standard multiplied by that percentage (e.g., 3 × .15 = .45). Adding the scores together provides us with a final average for the course on a four-point scale that colleges will accept.

Meets—4—vs. Exceeds—4*

Remember that we have changed the key for scoring from the model used in the younger grade levels. In this example, a 4 *meets* the standard and a 4* *exceeds* the standard, as shown in Figure 4.2.

Figure 4.2 Report Card Key

Key	
Standards-based scores are based on **end-of-year expectations.** Parenthetical numbers (e.g., (2)) indicate the goal for level of understanding at that point in the year. (N/A = not applicable)	4*—Exceeds expected level of understanding 4—Meets expected level of understanding consistently 3—Meets expected level of understanding, with support 2—Shows basic level of understanding 1—Shows basic level of understanding, with support
Soft skill scores identify the student's approach to learning and the learning environment. For example, a child may struggle with content but be very conscientious about the learning process.	E—**Exceeds** expectations M—**Meets** expectations R—Meets expectations, with **Reminders** S—**Struggles** to meet expectations

Let's look at a few other possibilities. Suppose Daniella was a strong English student who did well in her class. In Figure 4.3, we show her meeting the standards across the board.

Figure 4.3 Sample Grades for a Student with Uniform Strengths in English Class

Standard	4th Marking Period	%	Grade
RL.9–10. Key Ideas and Details	4(4)	10	.4
RI.9–10. Key Ideas and Details	4(4)	10	.4
RL & RI.9–10. Craft and Structure	4(4)	10	.4
RL.9–10. Integration of Knowledge and Ideas	4(4)	15	.6
RI.9–10. Integration of Knowledge and Ideas	4(4)	5	.2
W.9–10. Text Types and Purposes	4(4)	10	.4
W.9–10. Writing Skills	4(4)	15	.6
W.9–10. Research to Build Knowledge	4(4)	10	.4

Standard	4th Marking Period	%	Grade
SL.9–10. Present Ideas and Knowledge	4(4)	5	.2
L.9–10. Language and Vocabulary	4(4)	10	.4
	Final Average		**4.0**

A 4.0 makes sense, doesn't it? She actually mastered all of the standards set before her by the end of the year. Notice that I didn't say she was perfect. None of us are perfect. But in this case Daniella proved that she has a deep understanding of skill level at each standard. However, few students will actually demonstrate that level of proficiency with consistency. My Boy is a strong student who loves to read. Much to his English-teacher-father's chagrin, though, Xavier hates writing and often does just enough to get by. Therefore, his report card for English might look more like the example in Figure 4.4.

Figure 4.4 Sample Grades for a Student with Varied Strengths in English Class

Standard	4th MP	%	Grade
RL.9–10. Key Ideas and Details	4*(4)	10	.41
RI.9–10. Key Ideas and Details	4*(4)	10	.41
RL & RI.9–10. Craft and Structure	4*(4)	10	.41
RL.9–10. Integration of Knowledge and Ideas	4(4)	15	.6
RI.9–10. Integration of Knowledge and Ideas	4*(4)	5	.222
W.9–10. Text Types and Purposes	4(4)	10	.4
W.9–10. Writing Skills	3(4)	15	.45
W.9–10. Research to Build Knowledge	3(4)	10	.3
SL.9–10. Present Ideas and Knowledge	3(4)	5	.15
L.9–10. Language and Vocabulary	4(4)	10	.4
	Final Average		**3.752**

Notice the use of the 4* in this example. It indicates that the student has exceeded the set levels of expectation for that particular standard on a consistent basis. To account for this, the teacher "bumps" the grade by .1 for that standard (e.g., 4.1 × 10% = .41).

A FEW MORE CONSIDERATIONS

There are a few more items that must be considered with regard to the high school variation.

Avoiding Inflation

Perhaps the biggest concern in moving to this model is the very real potential for grade inflation. There is a way to avoid this, but it will take some significant planning and focus. We will discuss these structures in Chapter 7. For now, consider the benefits of the demonstrated structures: the focus remains on the learning throughout the year, and only the *learned* is used to identify a child's final average in a course.

Advanced Middle School

Many middle schools offer high school-level courses, such as algebra, for students who are ready to move forward in their learning, thereby necessitating a shift to the high school model for those courses. This could place two different grading systems in the same building: the model that places "meets expected level of understanding" at 3, and the model that places it at 4. A team may decide to shift the high school model described in this chapter to incorporate the middle school as well, though I would be hesitant about incorporating it below 7th grade. Instead, let the children continue to focus on the idea that school is more about learning than about grades for as long as possible.

Linear and Recursive Course Considerations

Some courses are more linear than others and therefore contain "one-and-done" concepts that are addressed within a marking period or two. A high school earth science course, for example, may have standards that address the workings of the universe during the first marking period and then not touch on those standards again for the rest of the school year. In such a case, these standards would be marked "not applicable" (N/A) for marking periods 2, 3, and 4. It is important that the student's grades for these standards be incorporated into the final average, as demonstrated in Figure 4.5.

Figure 4.5 Sample Report Card Using "Not Applicable" in Marking Periods, 2, 3, and 4

Marking Period		1	2	3	4	%	Grade
Earth Science	Student can:						
HS-ESS1–1	Demonstrate an understanding of the role of nuclear fusion at the sun's core.	3(4)	N/A	N/A	N/A	6	.18

Courses often have recursive elements in them as well. The same earth science course asks for students to model their learning, and such modeling is an important part of the Next Generation Science Standards. A teacher may *explicitly* instruct students in model development only during the first marking period, but over the course of the year the students will have many opportunities to practice and improve on the modeling skills. In such a case, the opportunity to continue to grow should be documented.

How well a student can use modeling to demonstrate a concept at the *end of the year* should determine her or his grade, no matter when the skill was initially taught.

End with a 4

Whether a standard is addressed in one marking period or four, at the high school level, the final parenthetical grade should **always** be a 4, as the 4 indicates that the expectation is that most students, most of the time, will meet the standard as appropriate for that grade level. We do not expect a 9th grade student to write as well as a 12th grade student, and the standards reflect that. Remember, the goal of a teacher is not to rank the students against each other, but to help the students meet the line established by the standards.

ACTION STEPS—HIGH SCHOOL

(continued from Chapter 2)

Step 8

At the fifth Foundation Team meeting:

- Review the rules for discussion and the role of the team.
- Remind the team of the current vision statement and modify, if necessary.
- Provide a sample section of the report card (such as the one shown in Figure 4.1), and ask Foundation Team members to dig into it. What do they like? What do they have questions about? What do they dislike?
- Discuss each part of the report card including clustered standards and the reasons to use them; parenthetical scores and how they relate to a student's actual score, as well as the reason to have them on the report card; soft skills; and the lack of a final average.
- Decide as a team which of these parts you will keep, and which, if any, you wish to discard.
- Define the scoring system numbers—4*, 4, 3, 2, 1.

- Decide whether the soft skills will be buildingwide or defined by grade. If the former, identify the soft skills that will be evaluated and the scoring system that will be used.
- Ask team members to spend some time thinking about a group that might be willing to try clustering standards before the next meeting.
- **Remind team members that they are free to talk about these discussions with other staff and in the community in order to get feedback.**

Step 9

Use the group's notes to develop a sample *blank* report card. There is no need to include the standards or grades. This is simply a visual representation of the work done to date.

Step 10

At the sixth Foundation Team meeting:

- Review the rules for discussion and the role of the team.
- Remind the team of the current vision statement and modify, if necessary.

NOTE

At this point the team should be comfortable with its vision statement. If there is still a need for significant change, stop here until the concerns have been addressed.

- Share the sample report card with the Foundation Team. What do team members like? Does anything need to be changed?
- Decide on a Trial Team that will experiment with completing the report card. This could be as simple as "English teachers"

or "social studies teachers" or "music teachers." This will go better if at least one member of the Foundation Team is on the Trial Team.

- Decide on the best way to approach the Trial Team and to introduce members to the changes that are being *considered* (remember, nothing is set in stone, yet). Set a time frame for getting that work done.
- **Remind team members that they are free to talk about these discussions with other staff and in the community in order to get feedback.**

Step 11

Approach the Trial Team and share the Foundation Team's work to date. Get a commitment from team members to complete the appropriate blank spaces in the sample report card.

- Set a time frame and ***provide time within the school day*** for the completion of the work.
- Ensure that Trial Team members understand that they have three responsibilities:
    —Develop standards-based clusters and place them on the sample report card;
    —Identify the parenthetical grades for each standard at each marking period using the definitions developed for 4*, 4, 3, 2, and 1 as a guide; and
    —Track the time it took to complete this work and any significant issues they had while working.
- Collect the completed work and associated notes.

- **Let Trial Team members know that they are free to talk about their work with other people on the staff and in the community in order to get feedback.**

Step 12

At the seventh Foundation Team meeting, review the work done by the Trial Team.

- Review the rules for discussion and the role of the team.
- Remind the team of the vision statement.
- Identify noted issues with the process. Are they reasonable, or do changes need to be made?
- Take note of the time needed to complete the task. Generally, the Trial Team is made up of willing participants. It may take other teams longer to do the same work. Use the Trial Team's notes as a yardstick in the future to plan for the work.
- **Remind team members that they are free to talk about these discussions with other staff and in the community in order to get feedback.**

5

Considerations That Affect Grading

Before we go any further with our planning, it is important that we come to a few understandings about what grading should look like in the classroom. Changing the grading system will not have the desired effect unless we can get everyone on board with these concepts. There are no action steps at the end of this chapter, as the concepts found here are built into the process as a whole.

HOMEWORK, PART 1

Harris Cooper (2015) documented the results of his homework meta-analysis in *The Battle over Homework*, a follow-up to his 1989 book, *Homework* (1989). Some key ideas to take away from his studies include:

- Homework in elementary school teaches kids to do homework, to study, and to organize their time. It has value for those reasons. It has little to no effect on their learning, so keep it short and practical.
- Homework at the middle school level supports learning, but if children have more than 90 minutes of homework a

night (total), their learning can actually diminish! Be certain that you are aware of the homework being assigned by other teachers. Collectively, try to avoid overwhelming the students.

- Homework at the high school level tends to improve learning without limit. However, I ask that you keep this in mind: as you sit at your kitchen table with a glass of wine, staring at the stack of papers that will take you two hours to grade, remember that your students won't have wine to help ease the pain. Be reasonable.

There are only three reasons to assign homework. The first is preparatory in nature. An art teacher might say, "Sketch your favorite place to sit. When you come in tomorrow, we will be using that sketch to explore methods of shading." An English teacher might ask students to read Poe's *The Masque of the Red Death* in order to discuss the concepts of mood and tone. The stipulation for preparatory homework is that the students can already do the work (e.g., sketch and read). They are not being asked to learn on their own.

The second reason to assign homework is for straight memorization (e.g., multiplication tables, poetry recitation, or phases of the moon).

The final reason to assign homework is so that it can be used as a formative assessment. In class, you teach, the students learn, you clarify, the students practice, you clarify further and you check for understanding. It seems that students have learned what you want them to learn. As a general rule of thumb, you can give "practice homework" when 80 to 100 percent of the students have demonstrated appropriate understanding in the classroom.

At this point, assign enough homework so that the students can demonstrate their knowledge or skill without your support. Don't give 20 problems when 5 will do. Homework is not a completion activity. It is a method for checking understanding.

HOMEWORK, PART 2

Not all students live in a home that is conducive to doing homework. Poverty exists in nearly every district in America. According to the U.S. Census Bureau, approximately 20 percent of the children in our country live below the poverty line (Proctor, Semega, & Kollar, 2016). Do all of the students in your class have a meal when they go home? Do they have running water? And poverty isn't the only issue. A child can come from a family that is well off, but not peaceful or attentive. Remember Maslow's hierarchy: if the child does not feel safe or loved, your social studies assignment will be way down on the list of "important stuff" in his or her brain.

There is a modicum of forgiveness built into the grading structure we are discussing because it does not tie completion rate to level of understanding. We should really make that forgiveness a standard of practice. If you know that a child has a difficult home life, what structures can be put into place that will allow her to complete the work in school? Ask yourself, "How can I ease the load?" If a child puts forth as much effort as can be expected given difficult circumstances, should she be given an "M" for "meets expectations" on her effort grade? These are critical discussions to have with one's colleagues.

Remember, too, that speed is not necessarily related to ability. If 10 questions are assigned in music theory, and one of your students only completes the first 6 of them, ask yourself, "Is she a slow reader?" "Does she struggle to write?" "How *well* did she answer those six questions?" Tie the work that she has completed to the standards and evaluate that—*not* her completion level.

HOMEWORK, PART 3

Allow students more than one attempt to demonstrate their learning. This book went through numerous iterations before it was even sent to the publisher. I have messed up the balance in my checkbook. I once called a new acquaintance "Bob" for an entire evening. His name is Jeremy. We all make mistakes. The key is acknowledging those mistakes and learning from them. What a wonderful message to impart to our students!

Moreover, allowing students to make mistakes and learn from them will probably decrease the instances of "alternate homework completion methods." Let's face it. We never know who is actually doing the homework. I copied about every third math homework assignment from my buddy Shannon when I was in high school. I have had parents say to me, "I hate the Common Core! I can't even do my 2nd grader's math!" My response was, "Why are you doing your 2nd grader's homework? What possible good will that do your child?"

Establish the following structure early—and be certain that all of your students (and their parents) understand it:

> If you put a *reasonable* amount of time and
> effort into an assignment and can't finish it
> or don't understand it, STOP! Let me know.

If one child is having an issue with an assignment, there's a good chance that others are as well. The onus for fixing that problem is on me—the teacher.

For younger children, a note from a guardian is fine. As the children get older, teach them to self-advocate. I would be thrilled if, instead of turning in a copy of her best friend's assignment, a student said to me, "Okay, Mr. Cornue. I spent 30 minutes staring at this stupid poem. I circled the figurative language. I looked for variations in rhyme scheme and rhythm. I have NO IDEA what this guy is talking about!"

GRADES CAN MEAN STOP

Paul Black and Dylan Wiliam (2001) have done a great deal of work on formative assessment, and I highly recommend that some time is spent reviewing their work. For our purposes, though, we should keep the following excerpt from "Inside the Black Box: Raising Standards through Classroom Assessment" in mind. When discussing structures that negatively affect student learning, they note that the following conditions are frequently found:

> The giving of marks and the grading func-
> tions are overemphasized, while the giving
> of useful advice and the learning function
> are underemphasized.

> Approaches are used in which pupils are compared with one another, the prime purpose of which appears to them to be competition rather than personal improvement. In consequence, assessment feedback teaches low-achieving pupils that they lack 'ability,' causing them to come to believe that they are not able to learn. (p. 84)

In other words, placing grades on the work of struggling students tends to make them think that they have finished their learning. For example, "If I receive a 2, then I am a 2 student when it comes to this topic." If, instead of a grade, we provide students with quality feedback on their assignments, projects, and homework, and if we provide them with an opportunity to improve upon their work, they are more likely to develop a growth mindset.

In short—we need to stop putting grades on everything that students turn in. Instead, provide them with quality feedback on their work and give them an opportunity to improve. This does not mean that you aren't tracking the grades in your books. It just means that a student does not always need to know what they are!

So what is "quality feedback"? Writing "Good job!" on an essay provides a student with no opportunity for growth or for the solidification of learning. "What did I do that was 'good'?" he may ask. "I would like to repeat that!" The phrase "Work harder!" elicits for me images of students screwing their faces up in effort. If a teacher instead writes, "Please pay more attention to the details in the text; they will help you better support your inferences," the student knows what he needs to do to improve.

Although it takes a bit longer, the mantra "Focused comments, fewer grades" will help students learn.

More recently, Dylan Wiliam (2016) has written about the benefits of having students do the evaluation of their own work. In his words, students need to do more of the "intellectual heavy lifting." This, of course, means that we have to explicitly teach them *how* to do this. This will take time at the outset, but will greatly benefit students in the long run.

The big idea behind all of this is simple: providing quality feedback (and asking students to be able to do the same) encourages personal growth over "grade-grubbing."

GROUP WORK AND GRADES

Paired and group learning are excellent structures. They help students learn to collaborate and communicate. They bring new ideas to the table and improve social skills. However, if a "group grade" is given, it is much more difficult to clearly identify what a student has learned. Instead, groups should work together, but students should have the opportunity to demonstrate their knowledge separately (O'Connor, 2007). (For a more complete exploration of this topic, check out the ASCD publication *Grading and Group Work: How do I assess individual learning when students work together?* by Susan M. Brookhart.)

INCOMPLETES VS. ZEROS

As a general rule of thumb, a score of zero should be avoided at all costs. A zero indicates that a child has not learned *anything* about the standard that is being addressed, and this is rarely the case. If a child does not turn in homework, we really don't know what his or her aptitude is in that standard. A zero gives that child permission to simply forget about completing the assignment. An "Incomplete" sets the expectation that the assignment *will* be completed so that the teacher can assess the learning (Dueck, 2014). Remember, when using the new report card system, we can always indicate that a student "struggles" with completing homework. That is enough.

6

Assignments, Assessments, and the Gradebook

The time from the beginning of this process until the beginning of its implementation will be at least two years. This cannot be emphasized enough. At this point, you have had about seven meetings (you can always add more, as needed) and have developed a knowledgeable Foundation Team. We have two more structural pieces to put into place before we roll this idea out to the rest of the stakeholders. The next part of the process is to build in the structures needed to track student work.

NOTE

From this point forward, "assignments" will be used to refer to homework, projects, in-class work, etc., and "assessments" will be used to refer to quizzes, tests, and the like. Let's remember, though, that every assignment should be used as a formative assessment!

TRACKING THE GROWTH

A gradebook, traditionally, provides a list of assignments and assessments followed by a student's grade for each. In this model, the gradebook is modified to address the student's learning and not the coupling of his or her completion rate with the learning. Consider Figure 6.1, which uses the EE math standard clusters identified in Chapter 3.

Figure 6.1 Traditional Gradebook Model Using EE Math Standard Clusters

	Homework #26	Quiz #4	Homework #27	Homework #28	Group Project #1	Unit Exam
Total points	**10**	**15**	**10**	**10**	**25**	**50**
Andrew	10	12	10	8	20	40
Jennifer	0	15	0	0	23	49
Sarah	7	10	7	7	20	38

What does this tell us? Andrew does pretty well, Sarah struggles a bit, and Jennifer doesn't do her homework though she knows the material very well, right? Of course the truth *could* be that Andrew could do much better but instead chooses to rest on his laurels, Jennifer is responsible for caring for two younger siblings while her single mother works the swing shift, and Sarah struggles with the material and is giving her best possible effort. Moreover, few of these grades give us much knowledge about the child's level of understanding for any particular topic.

In Figure 6.2, we use the four-point grading system and connect the grades to the standards as well as to the assignments and assessments. Take a few moments to review the set-up of this gradebook.

Figure 6.2 New Model for Tracking Student Growth

	Can show how arithmetic and algebra relate. (EE.6. Cluster A)				Understands one-variable equations and inequalities. (EE.6. Cluster B)				Can use dependent and independent variables to solve real-world problems. (EE.6. Cluster C)			
Assignments	H26 (3) / GP1 (3)	Q4 (3) / UE (3)	H27 (3)	H28	H26 / GP1 (3)	Q4 / UE (3)	H27 (2)	H28 (3)	H26 / GP1 (3)	Q4 / UE (3)	H27	H28 (2)
Andrew	3	3	4				2	3				3
	3	3			3	3			3	3		
	3								3			
Jennifer	Inc.	3	Inc.				Inc.	Inc.				Inc.
	(i)4	4			(i)3	4			(i)3	3		
	3	4							3			
Sarah	2	2	3				2	2				2
	3	3	(3)		2	2			2	2		
	2	3			2				2			

Note that:

- Homework assignment #26 and quiz #4 address only the first standard, homework assignment #27 addresses both the first and second standard, and so on.
- The parenthetical number after each assignment or assessment indicates the level of understanding or skill indicated by the successful completion of that task. For example, homework assignment #27 occurs after a few days of work on "Can show how arithmetic and algebra relate" (EE.6. Cluster A). At this point, the teacher expects the child to have this information mastered (3). On the other hand, this is the first homework assignment related to "Under-

stands one-variable equations and inequalities" (EE.6. Cluster B), and we have only just scratched the surface on the topic, so a 2 is appropriate for this score. Again, it is about the student's *understanding or skill in relation to the standard*. It is not about "completion."

- The (i) before each of Jennifer's group project grades indicates that she did not initially complete the work and received an "Incomplete." However, with some prompting and extra time, she did eventually get the work finished, as reflected by the grade.

- On the third line for each student, in italics, are additional grades based on one-to-one conversations and over-the-shoulder "peeks" as the students work in class. For each of these grades, which occur on an as-needed basis, the teacher asks, "What level of understanding is this child demonstrating regarding standard X?"

Were the grades placed on a traditional report card model, they would look like this:

- Andrew *83*
- Jennifer *73*
- Sarah *74*

A quick glance would tell me that both Andrew and Sarah have a better understanding of the standards than does Jennifer. And yet, we know that this is not the case.

In the new model (Figure 6.3), the scores are much more appropriate.

Figure 6.3 Sample of Standards-Based Report Card Scoring

Andrew:	
Can show how arithmetic and algebra relate.	3
Understands one-variable equations and inequalities.	3
Can use dependent and independent variables to solve real-world problems.	3
Jennifer:	
Can show how arithmetic and algebra relate.	4
Understands one-variable equations and inequalities.	4
Can use dependent and independent variables to solve real-world problems.	3
Sarah:	
Can show how arithmetic and algebra relate.	2
Understands one-variable equations and inequalities.	2
Can use dependent and independent variables to solve real-world problems.	2

The first concern a person may have with this system are the Incompletes (i) for Jennifer's homework. "She didn't do any of the homework. Even if I give her a 4 because she has the standards mastered, how can I justify that grade if she hasn't done all of the required work?"

We need to remember that these grades are based on student learning. If I know that Jennifer has a difficult home life, for example, homework may not be her top priority. However, I observe her taking notes and participating in class in order to ensure that she understands the learning. She can't get the homework done, but she has learned the information and skill. Her Effort grade may be an R (Meet expectations, with reminders), but I understand *why* this is the case and recognize that she is doing the best she can, given her circumstances. I should probably also ask myself, "How can I provide opportunities for Jennifer to complete the homework in school?"

If, on the other hand, Jennifer is simply choosing not to do her homework, I have some decisions to make. I may give her a different Effort grade. Is she an S (Struggles to meet expectations, even with reminders)? More importantly, I need to decide what to do about the problem. Is she not doing homework because she is bored with it? Do I need to better differentiate my instruction? Does she need more of a challenge?

The soft skills grades may seem relatively subjective here. That's because they are. They rely heavily on a teacher's professional judgment and knowledge of the students before them. However, using this model, this subjectivity no longer affects the grade that demonstrates a student's *understanding of the standard.*

ASSIGNMENTS AND ASSESSMENTS

A curriculum is based on standards. Therefore, the assignments and assessments within that curriculum should be based on standards, and a teacher should be able to explicitly identify which standards are being addressed in any given work that the students perform.

I remember (with some embarrassment) teaching Shakespeare's *Romeo and Juliet* to class after class of angst-y 9th graders. We slogged through it, focusing on understanding the words because, you know, Shakespeare. They need to read Shakespeare. I teach English, so I teach Shakespeare. Blech!

For grades 9 and 10, the English Language Arts Common Core State Standards ask that we "Analyze how an author draws on and transforms source material in a specific work (e.g., how

Shakespeare treats a theme or topic from Ovid or the Bible) or how a later author draws on a play by Shakespeare."

What if this standard was at my fingertips back then? Shakespeare wrote plays, not novels! They were meant to be seen! I could have shown a movie of the play, and then key scenes from *West Side Story*. Now we have an interesting discussion centered on Arthur Laurents's decisions with his play. For example, "In *Romeo and Juliet*, Romeo and Juliet both die at the end, but Laurents chooses to let Maria live after Tony has died. Why do you think he did that? How might it affect the play?" This can lead to other discussions on characterization, plot order, and the manipulation of time, all of which are parts of ELA Standard 5. The students end up reading Shakespeare to contribute to an interesting, *standards-based,* critical discussion—not simply because "We read Shakespeare in English."

Let's look at another example. Consider the assignment in Figure 6.4. The primary grade 6 Expressions and Equations grouping being addressed is Cluster C. However, in order to address the concept "Can use dependent and independent variables to solve real-world problems," the student must make use of the information learned in Clusters A and B. As a teacher, I have to decide which cluster or clusters (i.e., standards) I am going to be looking at for this assignment—and for every other assignment, quiz, exam, and project that I give. And my decision should coincide with that of every other teacher who teaches the same material.

While this may initially seem like lockstep instruction, understand that we are, at the moment, simply looking for common ground. Nothing in this model precludes a teacher from adding, removing, or changing an assignment in order to differentiate

---

Figure 6.4 Sample Homework Assignment with Standards References Added

Name:_____ Date:_____

Homework Assignment 14, Unit 4, Lesson 22

Grade Standard: 6EE

Clusters: A, B, and C

Level of understanding goals: 3, 3, and 3, respectively

Use tape diagrams to solve each problem.

A. Ed baked 60 cookies for this month's bake sale at his school, which is 10 more than he baked for last month's bake sale. Jody baked 20 more cookies this month than Maria baked. Jody baked the same number of cookies this month as Ed baked last month. Let e represent the number of cookies Ed baked last month and m represent the number of cookies Maria baked this month.

    1. How many cookies did Maria bake this month?

    2. What is the total number of cookies that Ed, Maria, and Jody baked for this month's bake sale?

B. Three girls on the school's basketball team scored a total of 50 points in last night's game. The number of points scored by Tracy was 10 fewer than the number of points scored by Liz. Melissa scored 3 times as many points as Tracy. Let the letter l represent Liz and the letter t represent Tracy.

    a. How many points did Liz score?

    b. How many points did Melissa score?

C. Kristin has 90 purses. Kristin has 12 fewer pairs of shoes than she has necklaces. If the number of purses Kristin has is double the number of necklaces she has, how many pairs of shoes does Kristin have? Let n represent the number of necklaces Kristin has and let s represent the number of pairs of shoes she has.

---

for her or his students *as it relates to the identified standards.* Nor does anything in the model prevent a teacher from instructing *beyond* the identified standards. If such changes are made, the structure remains the same. The teacher should be able to clearly identify the standards being taught and the levels of expectation.

DEVELOPING A SAMPLE

As with the development of the sample report card in Chapter 3, the talents of the Trial Team will be needed in order to develop a sample gradebook and a series of assignments and assessments to coincide with *one unit* of instruction. Team members should populate the gradebook with fictional names as well as with grades that approximate the work of an actual class of students. This model will be used as an example for the rest of the staff when the time comes.

As the Trial Team is looking at assignments and assessments, there is no need to reinvent the wheel! If an assignment already exists that addresses a particular concept found on the report card, the team should use it, tagging it with the appropriate standard. If a unit exam addresses four standards, the team may decide to reorganize the setup of the exam in order to clump like standards together so that they will be easier to assess, but there is no need to rewrite every question.

Also, remind the Trial Team that different assignments may demonstrate different levels of understanding, as seen in Figure 6.2. For example, a student who completes a biology assignment in which she has correctly *identified* all of the steps in the process of mitosis still only has a cursory 2 level of understanding of the process. It may take a week or more before a child can *explain* the process of mitosis, which would indicate mastery of the standard. At the top of the assignment in Figure 6.4, the standards addressed and the expected levels of understanding are clearly indicated.

Once the assignments and assessments are developed and keyed into the gradebook, and after a sample class with sample grades is entered into it, the Trial Team should use those grades to appropriately fill in the report card sample.

This is long and difficult work, and a "thank you" gift for the Trial Team may be warranted, but the Foundation Team now has in its hands an exemplar of the assignments, assessments, gradebook, and report card. These will be invaluable tools when it comes to planning and to bringing the rest of the staff along.

METHODS FOR DEVELOPMENT

At this time, there is no quick and easy computer program for the development of a physical gradebook, though anyone with a decent grasp of Microsoft Excel should be able to set up a working structure using the model displayed earlier in this chapter. The basic outline for this model should be created by the Foundation Team before handing it off to the Trial Team. Please note that in the sample in Figure 6.2, the standards and assignments are both at the top of the page and the student names are on the left. In Excel, this will allow the teacher to "lock" those rows and column so that they are always visible.

(To download the sample gradebook model I developed, go to http://bit.ly/CornueGradebook (case-sensitive).)

ACTION STEPS

(continued from Chapter 3)

Step 13

At the eighth Foundation Team meeting:

- Review the rules for discussion and the role of the team.
- Remind the team of the current vision statement.
- Provide a sample section of the gradebook and ask Foundation Team members to dig into it. What do they like? What do they have questions about? What do they dislike?
- Discuss each part of the gradebook. Note that the standards, the assignment references, and the parenthetical expected levels of understanding *in relation to the standard* are at the top.
- Decide as a team which of these parts you will keep, and which, if any, the team wishes to discard.
- Assign someone to develop the gradebook model in Excel or a similar program and to enter the standards identified on the sample report card into the spreadsheet. Alternatively, the team may choose to use or modify the one I developed.

- **Remind team members that they are free to talk about these discussions with other staff and in the community in order to get feedback.**

Step 14

Approach the Trial Team and share the Foundation Team's work to date.

Ensure that Trial Team members understand all parts of the report card.

- Set a time frame and *provide time within the school day* for the completion of the work.
- Ensure that Trial Team members understand that they have five responsibilities:
  — Connect and adjust, as necessary, their assignments and assessments from **one unit** to the standards they identified for the sample report card;
  — Identify the parenthetical level of expected learning for each assignment;
  — Develop a mock class with mock grades;
  — Use those grades to fill in the sample gradebook; and
  — Track the time it took to complete this work and list significant concerns.
- Collect the completed work and associated notes.
- **Remind team members that they are free to talk about these discussions with other staff and in the community in order to get feedback.**

Step 15

At the ninth Foundation Team meeting, review the work done by the Trial Team.

- Identify noted issues with the process. Are they reasonable, or do changes need to be made?
- Take note of the time needed to complete the task.

NOTE

Again, the Trial Team is generally made up of willing participants. It may take other teams longer to do the same work. In the future, use the Trial Team's notes as a yardstick to plan for the work.

- **Remind team members that they are free to talk about these discussions with other staff and in the community in order to get feedback.**

7

Timeline, Avoiding Grade Inflation, and Decision Time

Let's take a few moments to review what has been accomplished thus far.

A Foundation Team has been gathered to study grading and scoring. Team members recognize that most traditional systems are unfair in that they inaccurately connect effort and behaviors to an understanding of the standards that are being evaluated. The team acknowledges that standards-based grading provides all stakeholders with more information than a single, all-encompassing grade. Team members know that averaging the learning instead of identifying the learned is illogical, and that averaging the standards is simply an unnecessary step until high school. They know that grading should be used to support learning, not to judge students or to rank them against each other.

A four-point system (with a .1 bump (4*) in high school) has been developed with a clear guide that identifies each level of understanding, and Foundation Team members understand that these scores do not correlate with traditional models. In other words, a 4 does not equal an *A* or 90–100; instead, they connect to the standards. Separate guides have been developed to address soft skills so that they can be tracked without interfering with the record of a student's grasp of or skill at meeting a standard. The Trial Team has developed a matching gradebook and report card with a mock-up of grades tied to sample assignments and assessments. These latter items are directly connected to the standards that have been selected for the report card, and the appropriate level of understanding that each evaluates is identified by marking period. The work completed by the Trial Team has been timed.

We have our in-house experts. We have examples of the work. We have an estimate of the time it will take to complete the work. Now comes the hard work.

TIMELINE, PART 1

The work we have already addressed should take no more than a year to complete. Any more than that, and there is a chance that it will fall off the radar or be replaced by some new initiative. If started in August or September, the goal should be to share the Foundation Team's plans with the rest of the staff by the penultimate month of the same school year. And when it is shared, an appropriate timeline should be included in the planning.

In speaking with teachers, principals, central office administrators, and state officials during and after New York's recent changes in standards and teacher evaluation structures, the most frequent complaint I heard was that the changes were rolled out too fast. On the other hand, just setting a general deadline way out at some future date usually ensures that there is a frantic rush to begin and finish the project in the last three months. There needs to be a structure to this change.

Remember, to make the changes in grading and scoring, every educator will need to:

1. *Change the classroom grading models and report cards.* This includes identifying which standards (or parts of standards, or combined standards) will be evaluated, and when and how those standards will be evaluated. It also includes creating rubrics, evaluating and modifying assignments and assessments, and changing gradebooks (or the electronic equivalent). Teachers also will need time for development of these items. And that means that the district will have to provide summer-work opportunities or staff days during the year for joint planning.

2. *Implement the changes.* The first year of implementation will have its issues. Time needs to be set aside for teachers and administrators to problem solve.

This chapter includes two possible schedules for making the changes in grading and scoring. Look to your own staff and school structures to decide which of these makes the most sense for your organization. These plans are designed for districtwide change, but can be modified to a school.

NOTE
Each plan begins in Year 2 as the timelines begin after the Foundation Team and Trial Team have completed their work.

Structure 1: The Five- to Seven-Year Plan

Changes are made with smaller cohorts.

Year 2

Development. The first round of teachers involved in the change will begin to plan. Standards will be identified, gradebooks and report cards will be developed, and assignments, assessments, and rubrics will be modified or developed as necessary and connected to levels of expectation. This first group will be grades PreK–2 (if appropriate), the first year of middle school (depending on the district, this is usually grade 5, 6, or 7), and grade 9.

Year 3

Implementation. The first round of teachers implements the change.

Development. The second round of teachers (grade 3, the second year of middle school, and grade 10) will begin their planning.

Year 4

Implementation. The second round of teachers implements the change.

Development. The third round of teachers (grade 4, the third year of middle school where appropriate, and grade 11) will begin their planning.

Year 5

Implementation. The third round of teachers implements the change.

Development. The fourth round of teachers (grade 5 where appropriate, the fourth year of middle school where appropriate, and grade 12) will begin their planning.

Year 6

Implementation. The fourth round of teachers implements the change.

Development. The fifth round of teachers (grades 6, where appropriate, and grade 12) will begin their planning.

Year 7

Implementation. The fifth round of teachers implements the change.

Structure 2: The Four-Year Plan

Larger cohorts are addressed.

Year 2

Development. The first round of teachers involved in the change will begin to plan. Standards will be identified, gradebooks and report cards will be developed, and assignments, assessments, and rubrics will be modified or developed as necessary and connected to levels of expectation. This first group will be the first years of elementary school (e.g., grade PreK–2), the first years of middle school (e.g., grades 5 and 6), and the first years of high school (e.g., grades 9 and 10).

Year 3

Implementation. The first round of teachers implements the change.

Development. The second round of teachers at the elementary, middle, and high school (the final years of elementary school, the final years of middle school, and the final years of high school) will begin their planning.

Year 4

Implementation. The second round of teachers implements the change.

Be aware that a four-year "quick change" to the grading model suggested in this book could be problematic at the high school level. The district would have to take a close look at how transcripts would be addressed if half of the grades follow a traditional model, and half follow the new model. It may make sense to follow the first structure for the high school and the second structure for the rest of the buildings.

TEACHERS OF MULTIPLE GRADES

The Foundation Team should work closely with those teachers who teach multiple grade levels to determine how best to make the change in their subjects. For example, when using the four-year plan, an elementary music teacher who teaches grade levels PreK–5 may decide that it is easier for him to follow the same model: PreK–2 in the first year of development, and 3–5 in the second. On the other hand, the district may not have the resources to include everyone at once, and may tack on an extra year to address physical education, chorus, band, music, art, and the like.

THE ONE- AND 13-YEAR PLANS

The plans I have provided are just suggestions, but they are reasonable in their scope. What I recommend against is the "one-year plan" because it would be too overwhelming, and the

"13-year plan" because I have my doubts about any organization's ability to sustain focus for such an extended period of time.

TIMELINE, PART 2

Identifying the length of time it will take to make the change is only the first part of the timeline process. Careful thought also needs to go into planning *when* the work will get done within that time frame.

To do this, the Foundation Team should go back to the notes of the Trial Team. How long did it take the Trial Team to identify the standards and set up one part of the report card? Use that as a guide to identify the number of days (yes, days) it will take for a team to do the same for an entire report card. There are a number of questions to answer about this process:

- When will those meetings occur?
- How will they be structured?
- What support will the teachers have in the development process?
- What secretarial support do they need?

Then follow the same format to decide how long it will take and in what manner each cohort of teachers will address gradebooks, assignments, and assessments.

From these details, a timeline with specific action steps should be developed. Dates, times, and expectations for each cohort of teachers (e.g., grade 8 social studies) need to be placed on a calendar so that arrangements can be made for a space to work, clerical support (if needed), substitute teachers (if needed), and a Foundation Team or Trial Team member to help guide the process (if needed). A template of the report card and gradebook should be placed on a common server so that teachers can make a copy of each for their own use.

AVOIDING GRADE INFLATION

A final measure needs to be addressed when developing the timeline. Teachers need time to sit down together with samples of their students' work. They need to discuss why paper x is a 2 and paper y is a 3. In Chapter 5 I mentioned that there is a way to avoid grade inflation. This is it. If, once a month, everyone in a cohort brings a sample of a 1, a 2, a 3, and a 4 (and a 4*, in high school) on a common assignment to a meeting of like teachers, they can be certain that the grading model they are using is relatively universal. This approach also keeps us from being too rough on the students as we are grading.

Generally, these meetings work best if a single teacher for each group takes on the role of facilitator. That does not mean that they are always right! A facilitator's job is simply to choose the assignment that will be discussed, and to keep the meeting focused on the task at hand: "Bob scored this paper a 2 as it relates to standard x. Let's all take a look at it and see if we agree."

After a year or so of monthly meetings, the teachers may not need to gather quite so frequently, but these discussions need to become an integral part of the process. Never should a year go by without at least quarterly meetings to share exemplars and ensure that everyone is scoring student work similarly. Such meetings need to be integrated into the yearly calendar.

ACTION STEPS

(continued from Chapter 6)

Step 16

At the 10th Foundation Team meeting:

- Review the rules for discussion and the role of the team.
- Remind the team of the current vision statement.
- Discuss potential completion timelines for the change, and agree on the one that makes the most sense for your district or building.
- Develop a schedule for the change, using the timing notes gathered by the Trial Team for guidance.
- Develop times for cohorts to meet and share student work after implementation.
- **Remind team members that they are free to talk about these discussions with other people on the staff and in the community in order to get feedback.**

Decision time

At this point, all of the foundational work has been completed. Your group of experts has seen why the change is needed and has a plan to make the change. Acknowledge that there will be hiccups along the way, and that there will be unexpected elements that need to be addressed. Remind the team that up to this point, the process has been purely exploratory. And then ask the question: are we going to move forward with this process, or are we going to keep our grading system the same as it has been?

If the Foundation Team has been empowered to make the decision, allow for some brief discussion, and then take a vote. If the Foundation Team is advisory, ask for members' opinions, and then make a decision.

Step 17

At the 11th Foundation Team meeting:
- Review the rules for discussion and the role of the team.
- Remind the team of the current vision statement.
- Make a decision.
- **Ask team members to hold off on spreading news of the decision until an appropriate method for doing so can be decided upon.**

8

Getting Buy-In

THE BOARD OF EDUCATION

The district's board of education, as mentioned in Chapter 2, should be made aware of the exploration into changing the grading model from the outset. How often the board is updated on the process is up to the district. You know your people. After the decision is made to move forward with the process, many districts will require board approval. Be certain to factor this in early enough to be placed on the board's agenda. Choose a presentation team and decide on the best format to demonstrate the importance of the shift to a new grading model. Be sure to emphasize the "why"! Show the work that has been done to prepare for the implementation.

THE TEACHERS

Once the board has approved the change, the Foundation Team needs to develop a plan for encouraging staff buy-in. Some decisions need to be made. Who will present the information? Ideally, an administrator and a teacher or two (maybe the "respected elder" or the "group cynic"?) will copresent the information to the staff. How will the information be presented? Will a PowerPoint be used? A position paper? Who will create and write the material? Will it be presented to the staff as a whole or to smaller groups?

However the team decides to present the information, it should be offered to the staff no later than the second-to-last month of the school year, and the attendees should be informed that they will be given a few weeks to process the information before a final meeting, at which time additional questions will be addressed. This discussion should come as a surprise to no one, as nearly every list of Action Steps in the previous chapters ends with this statement: **Remind team members that they are free to talk about these discussions with other staff and in the community in order to get feedback.** This gathering is not supposed to shock the audience. Rather, it should be an information session. Be sure to include:

- The vision statement.
- The names of the people on the team.
- An explanation of the research done.
- A clear list of the reasons that a change needs to occur.
- The specific steps necessary to complete the change, along with the sample assignments, assessments, gradebook, and report card section.
- Some of the big ideas associated with the change, including no averaging—we trust each teacher's judgment; not every assignment needs a grade on the paper; and push for growth, not "grade-grubbing."
- The timeline for the change.

Once staff members know that the change is going to happen, they need a chance to have their voices heard. Give them a month or so to contemplate and discuss the change. Make the vision statement and the library of resources available to them. Let them ask questions of the Foundation Team and Trial Team. Then meet one final time before the end of the school year to address any pressing questions or concerns.

Oh, and remember that change is hard. Be patient.

THE COMMUNITY

Early on in this process, community members should have received a letter from the district, informing them of the exploration of a new grading system. Now it is time to let them know that the change will occur. A letter that explains the "why" and that provides samples of the new report card is probably the best initial approach. Be certain that it includes an example or two for high school and middle school, as the parents of these students will be most concerned about any model that may directly affect their children's future options.

In addition to providing an explanation of the report card, focus on the *reasons* for the system change:

- It is fair to students.
- It allows students to make mistakes and learn from them without being penalized for going through the learning process.
- It separates behavior and expectations from the learning itself.

In short, it provides valuable information and a usable structure to the teachers, parents, and the children themselves in order to better facilitate learning.

A public forum may also be necessary. I recommend that forums be handled building-by-building, with the same Foundation Team member or members present at each of them for support. (Having the same person attend each meeting helps minimize the chances of mixed messages.)

In addition, I recommend that such meetings be held off until at least the second semester of the first planning year. Give staff members an opportunity to dig into the process a bit. The stronger their understanding, the better they can support the change. Remember, teachers are the most reachable ambassadors for the parents and students. Their support is key!

TECHNOLOGY AND THE REPORT CARD

Many schools now provide online versions of report cards, and even, in some cases, teachers' gradebooks. While I am unaware of a program that currently would support the model discussed in this book, this does not mean that one cannot be found or created. Don't let technology drive the grading. Instead, start conversations with your technology providers early in the process.

ACTION STEPS

(continued from Chapter 7)

Step 18

At the 12th Foundation Team meeting:
- Review the rules for discussion and the role of the team.
- Remind the team of the current vision statement.
- Develop a presentation for the board of education.
- Choose a point of contact to place the group on the board's agenda.
- Establish times for the presenters to *practice*!

Step 19

At the 13th Foundation Team meeting:
- Review the rules for discussion and the role of the team.
- Remind the team of the current vision statement.
- Develop a presentation for the staff (base it on the board of education presentation to save time), and select the presenters if they will be different.
- Establish times for the presenters to *practice*!

- Choose a date and time for the first presentation and choose someone to ensure that the rest of the staff will be present.
- Brainstorm ideas for the community letter and select one or two people to write a draft. Ask them to send a copy of the draft to the other members of the Foundation Team for comment.

Step 20

Introduce the change to the Board of Education, then to staff.

Step 21

At the 14th Foundation Team meeting:
- Review the rules for discussion and the role of the team.
- Remind the team of the current vision statement.
- Finalize the letter to the community.
- Identify the person who will see to the letter's distribution, following district guidelines.

Step 22

Hold a second staff meeting about one month later to answer questions and address concerns. If you want to "cheat" a little, ask staff members to send their thoughts ahead of time and schedule another Foundation Team meeting to brainstorm answers.

Step 23

Establish dates for community forums if it seems that they will be needed.

9

The Development Teams

Schools should now be ready to begin the work of changing their grading systems. Let's call each cohort of teachers responsible for doing the work necessary to implement the changes a Development Team. Depending on the district, this may involve either summer work or planning time during the regular school year. In either case, it will be important to set concrete dates and times when the Development Team members can work together. These sessions should be held sacrosanct. Too often, something "comes up" to pull a teacher away from such meetings. I would go so far as to recommend an alternate location for the work. A 3rd grade Development Team, for example, is much less likely to be disturbed or distracted if members meet in a high school building.

ORGANIZING DEVELOPMENT TEAM MEETINGS

If you work in a small district with only two or three teachers per grade level or topic, these meetings may be easy to organize. Everyone who will be affected can be involved in the decision-making process. If, though, there are a large number of teachers responsible for a particular grade, gathering them all together is impractical. In such a case, the temptation may be to stack the deck. You know which teachers are "open" and willing to do the work. But you should also include people who may be hesitant about the change. Let them be won over through the process and discussions.

Each Development Team should have a Foundation Team member, a Trial Team member, or both, as its go-to person for questions. As appropriate, special education teachers, support staff, or both, should be represented on the Development Teams. Once the materials are developed, team members should share them with the appropriate personnel for commentary and suggestions, and then make revisions as necessary.

FOLLOWING THE TRIAL TEAM PATTERN

Each Development Team should follow the pattern used by the Trial Team. Begin by identifying the standards that will be evaluated, as well as the expected levels of performance by marking period. Teams should be reminded that the standards are year-end goals and that not every standard needs to be addressed in every marking period. Once this work is completed, it should be submitted electronically for easy transfer to the report card model.

Next, the team needs to address its existing assignments and assessments, clearly identifying the standard or standards being addressed in each. Finally, the gradebook should be set up, providing enough spaces in each marking period for the standards being evaluated and for the assignments connected to those standards (as seen in Chapter 6). Once again, in larger districts, those not directly involved in the process should have the opportunity to comment and make suggestions before the final work is completed.

The remainder of this chapter breaks down this process into more detail.

THE REPORT CARD

When developing the report card, the teams should be provided with specific, written guidance and exemplars to facilitate their work. An example is provided in Figure 9.1. After the report card is developed, it should be shared with all of the other teachers of the same grade level or subject to allow them an opportunity to provide feedback and suggestions. Those suggestions should be carefully considered by the Development Team so that any final changes can be made.

NOTE

Generally, one or two people should be responsible for developing the structure of the report card for the entire district (see Appendix B for two report card samples). These people will also work with the technology specialists, as necessary. All of the pieces of the report card that the Development Teams create should be submitted to this person for the sake of uniformity.

NOTE

Teachers may wish to add a "Comments" section to the report card. Certainly, this is a viable option that should be considered, as it can give more details about a student's growth.

Figure 9.1 Sample Directions for Report Card Planning

Report Card Guidance

Grading Vision Statement: We believe schools are about teaching and learning and that the grading system should be consistent for all learners. We believe a good reporting system accurately communicates to the students, parents, and school both the growth and level of student learning.

Dear 6th Grade Teachers:

In order to shift our grading system, we are asking that you identify those items that you feel would inform the child's parents and future teachers. To do this, follow these steps:

1. Consider all of the standards that you teach over the course of the year.

2. Choose those standards that are addressed fully enough or that are important enough to warrant space on the report card. (Note: This does NOT mean that those standards left off the list will be ignored.)

3. Compile standards where appropriate in order to limit the number of individual items being evaluated to 20 or fewer for the entire year.

4. Reword those standards into brief, parent-friendly language. For example: "*Apply and extend previous understandings of multiplication and division to divide fractions by fractions,*" becomes "*Understands fraction division and why it works.*"

5. Identify the marking period(s) in which each standard will be addressed.

6. Identify the level of learning that can be expected from *most students, most of the time,* in each marking period in which a standard is taught, evaluated, or both. Remember that the goal is a level 3 understanding for most standards by the *end of the year.*

7. Chart your work as demonstrated below and submit a digital copy to _____.
   A blank copy of the chart can be found at _____. The chart is due by the end of the day on _____.

A separate chart should be completed for each subject. Please address the subjects in this order: math, ELA, science, social studies.

Standard and Reference	MP	Level
Can show how arithmetic and algebra relate. (EE.6 Cluster A)	1	2
	2	3
	3	3
	4	3
Understands one-variable equations and inequalities. (EE.6 Cluster B)	1	N/A
	2	2
	3	3
	4	3

Thank you for your time and hard work!

ASSIGNMENTS AND ASSESSMENTS

Once the report card is firmly established, the same process needs to be followed for modified assignments or assessments and for the gradebook model. Exemplars should be provided, along with specific guidance directing teachers to:

1. Tie all assessments and assignments to a standard or to multiple standards that will be evaluated on the report card. Ideally, these should be listed at the top of each assignment, as demonstrated in Figure 6.4.
2. Identify the marking period in which each assignment or assessment will be used.
3. These items should also be given a name to key them to the gradebook, such as Homework 12 (H12) or Quiz 22 (Q22). This will help teachers keep track of owed work (Figure 6.2).
4. Provide a count of the number of times each standard will be assessed in each marking period. This will be very important when it comes to developing the gradebook.

Once again, I am not suggesting "lock-step" instruction. However, major assignments and assessments are often common across a topic. The short-story unit exam is probably the same in Grade 9 Classroom A and in Grade 9 Classroom B. If a teacher has a different take on student learning—say, she uses a different text to teach the same concept, and therefore has assessment materials that are different from her colleagues—that's fine. She may just have to set up the tracking for those materials on her own, but the addressed standards would remain the same.

THE GRADEBOOK

The gradebook model shown in Figure 6.2 provides room for six grades per standard, which is generally too few for most marking periods. As previously mentioned, you are free to use the blank gradebook model I developed and posted online. It was developed in Microsoft Excel with space for 12 standards per marking period, 20 assignments and assessments per standard, and 35 students. There are 30 spaces for grades in each standard for each student. The first two rows correspond to the assignments and assessments. Numbers in the bottom rows are italicized and provide an opportunity to record additional evaluations that may be found through conversations, support work, and "over-the-shoulder" observations.

Teachers should use this model, or one developed by the district, to enter the standards they choose for the report card, as well as the corresponding assignment and assessment numbers and the expected level of learning for each (e.g., HW27 [2]).

STATING THE OBVIOUS

There is a fair amount of work involved in this process. It is important that the Development Teams understand that all of the elements need to be completed by a set date. When provided with the scheduled working dates at the beginning of the process, the team members can better plan their time.

AN ALTERNATE MODEL

Earlier in this chapter, I recommended addressing the report card as a whole before moving on to the assignments, assessments, and gradebook. However, there is no reason a district cannot address all of these parts for one particular subject, and then repeat the process for subsequent subjects. For example, develop the report card structures, assignments, assessments, and gradebook for math, and then do the same for ELA, science, and so on. Find the model that works best for your people.

ACTION STEPS

(continued from Chapter 8)

Step 24

At the 15th Foundation Team meeting:
- Review the rules for discussion and the role of the team.
- Remind the team of the current vision statement.
- Review and make adjustments to the timeline developed in Action Step 16, if necessary.
- Identify the members of each Development Team.
- Identify the locations in which the Development Teams will work.
- Identify the Foundation Team or Trial Team member who will support each Development Team.
- Create guidance documents for the Development Teams and place them with the exemplars.
- Identify the *report card guru*.
- Distribute the timeline to the Development Teams, which will first make the change to the new grading system.
- Get the work started!

Step 25

Support the work and develop the report card.

Step 26

Distribute the report card to all those it will affect for commentary and suggestions. Have Development Team members adjust the report cards as necessary and finalize the report card.

Step 27

Distribute modified assignments and assessments to all teachers they will affect. Remind them that they are not "stuck" with these changes. Modifications and adjustments to meet the needs of the students are a part of teaching!

Step 28

Provide the completed gradebook—with standards, assignments, assessments, and expectations entered—to the teachers who will be using it, along with instructions for its use.

10

Critical Notes

FOLLOW-THROUGH

Part of the process for building to a successful change is the follow-through, and follow-through is something that many of us tend to, well, let's say, "let slide" in our everyday lives.

Over the past 16 years, The Bride and I (with a great deal of help from my father!) have been turning our 150-year-old ramshackle house into a home. We've rewired, torn down and replaced walls, repaired plumbing, refinished floors, painted, and tried to ignore the fact that it is impossible to find a square corner anywhere in the place. One piece that I always struggle with is the detail work. The new walls are up and painted in our bedroom, the mopboard is in place, and even the quarter-round shoe has been installed. All that needs to be done is a little filling and staining with wood putty in the gaps on the trim work (did I mention the lack of a square corner in the house?). But that's boring stuff. That's tedious. And unless you look closely, you won't notice it.

Unless, of course, you are visiting. You see, I stop noticing those gaps because I am there every day. It's just "the house."

But someone who isn't there as frequently may see that the work isn't done. It stands out in an otherwise finished room.

I'm fortunate in that The Bride is detail oriented. She doesn't let me get away with ignoring the seemingly insignificant elements that complete the final product. I'm ready to tear down walls in the next room because it is new and exciting, but she points me back to the work that needs to be finished.

Be certain that you have a similarly detail-oriented person in your corner when you begin work on the new grading system.

During year three of the change, the second cohort of teachers will complete their planning while the first cohort of teachers begins to implement the new grading system. This means that a great deal of focus and a large number of the available resources will be geared toward the second cohort. However, as explained at the end of Chapter 7, it will be critical that the first cohort of teachers have time to sit down together at least once a month so that they can develop a sense of scoring agreement and make adjustments to their plans as they move forward.

Consider, too, how the new grading model will be introduced to incoming teachers and administrators. Who will present them with the new model? Who will support them as they transition to something entirely different? How will you "sell them" on moving beyond compliance and into belief in the system? These structures should be part of a written plan that is implemented whenever new staff members come on board.

SPECIAL EDUCATION

When speaking of special education students, most educators will place the children into two categories: those with severe cognitive delays, and everyone else. Generally, the former group of students receives "alternate assessments" and is held to different standards. The latter group—the much *larger* group—of special education students is expected to be provided with **meaningful** access to the same standards as their peers.

To be clear: a child's individualized education plan (IEP) requires accommodations, modifications, or both, and it is our responsibility to use those structures to help that child meet grade-level standards at the same level as his or her non-IEP peers. The report card doesn't change.

Concerns may be raised about the effect this could have on special education students who continue to struggle. There are those educators who, under a different grading system, might be tempted to "boost" a grade because a student has shown "significant growth" or "good effort"; they don't want the child to become discouraged by the grade. This is a laudable intent, but we need to categorize the strengths appropriately. A student can have 1s and 2s next to the standards, and an "M" (Usually Meets Expectations) in the Effort category related to soft skills. In a discussion with my colleague Kristin Capotosto (2016, personal interview), the New York State Central Regional Special Education Training Specialist (RSETS), I was also reminded that the progress-monitoring associated with IEP goals is designed to identify growth. Those reports, as well as the IEP, go hand in glove with the report card. Adding the same information to the report card would be redundant.

GUIDANCE COUNSELORS

Early on in this text, I recommended that the Foundation Team should include a guidance counselor. The input of guidance counselors throughout the process will be valuable, but it is as the new grading model is being implemented that they become absolutely imperative.

The guidance department should have a deep understanding of the changes being made, as this will help counselors place students in the appropriate classes. If a counselor doesn't understand that a collection of 3s and 4s, for example, indicates that a child is probably navigating grade 5 math with ease and aplomb, he or she may not consider placing that child in an honors math class.

Equally important is the shift at the high school level. High school counselors may need to take time to draft a letter to supplement the transcript, explaining the new model of grading, its similarity to the standard 4.0 system used by the colleges, and the manner by which students who excel at a particular concept are identified and "bumped up." A similar letter should be sent to the admissions officers of those colleges the district's students most frequently attend in order to give them a heads up. It may be worthwhile to host a meeting with those admissions officers in order to answer any questions.

THE MENTAL SHIFT

The work is completed. The Foundation Team spent a year studying and planning. Another year was spent by the members of the first cohort to identify their standards, adjust their materials, and create their gradebooks. We are finally ready to do—what, exactly?

With all the intricacies and paperwork and planning, it can be easy to overlook what the actual expectations are, so let's lay them out in their simplest form:

- Teachers will help students learn.
- Teachers will record student understanding, based on the standards, using an agreed-upon four-point scale (with a .1 bump (4*) in high school).
- Teachers will use their **informed professional judgment,** NOT an average, to determine a score for the identified standards in each marking period.
- Teachers will use their **informed professional judgment** to share "soft-skill" information about a student for each subject.

That's it. Once the process is set up, the rest is simply teaching and evaluating, as teachers have always done. The results *look* different, because the grades are more useful, but the process of getting to them remains the same.

"If such is the case," some may ask, "why make the change at all?"

Remember the "why"?

Here's the elevator speech:

> Our current grading system combines a student's understanding of multiple ideas and skills into a single grade. Moreover, it often includes variances based on behavior, organizational abilities, teacher expectation, and other elements that have little to do with the standards. The new grading model

helps us to separate these soft skills from student understanding. It also helps us break a single grade for a huge topic, like U.S. History and Government, into multiple grades for smaller component pieces like "how reform efforts affect both economics and social order." This provides teachers with better information about where a child is experiencing success and where additional support may be needed. Finally, the new grading model uses a 1–4 system because that is all we need. The student is struggling toward, getting closer to, has achieved understanding of, or has gone beyond the standard. Oh—and we got rid of averaging because it is illogical.

Okay. So the elevator needs to be traveling at least 10 floors to fit that all in, but you get the idea. And everyone else in the building should, too—as should the parents, the students, and the community at large. This is the mental shift. This may also be a *cultural* shift, placing the focus of the grades on the learned and the focus of the teachers on the learning instead of on the grades. Don't jump to this model because it is the new thing. Don't use the new gradebook because the school says you have to. The constant reminder that needs to be shared is this:

Make this change because this model helps us better focus on student growth and learning, and that is truly our end goal.

ACTION STEPS

(continued from Chapter 9)

Step 29

At the 16th Foundation Team meeting:
- Review the rules for discussion and the role of the team.
- Remind the team of the current vision statement.
- Establish a calendar for grade- or subject-level teams to meet at least once a month to build scoring agreement as they evaluate student work, and develop guidelines for the meetings.

Step 30

At the 17th Foundation Team meeting:
- Review the rules for discussion and the role of the team.
- Remind the team of the current vision statement.
- Work with the guidance department to develop an explanatory letter that can be attached to student transcripts and sent to select colleges.
- If necessary, work with the guidance department to host a meeting with the admissions officers of frequently attended colleges to answer questions about the new system.

And...

Preach the benefits of the change—often!

Appendix A: Common Core Mathematics Standards—Grade 6

Ratios & Proportional Relationships 6.RP

Understand ratio concepts and use ratio reasoning to solve problems.

1. Understand the concept of a ratio and use ratio language to describe a ratio relationship between two quantities. *For example, "The ratio of wings to beaks in the bird house at the zoo was 2:1, because for every 2 wings there was 1 beak." "For every vote candidate A received, candidate C received nearly three votes."*

2. Understand the concept of a unit rate a/b associated with a ratio a:b with b ≠ 0, and use rate language in the context of a ratio relationship. *For example, "This recipe has a ratio of 3 cups of flour to 4 cups of sugar, so there is 3/4 cup of flour for each cup of sugar." "We paid $75 for 15 hamburgers, which is a rate of $5 per hamburger."* (Expectations for unit rates in this grade are limited to noncomplex fractions.)

3. Use ratio and rate reasoning to solve real-world and mathematical problems (e.g., by reasoning) about tables of equivalent ratios, tape diagrams, double number line diagrams, or equations.

    a. Make tables of equivalent ratios relating quantities with whole-number measurements, find missing values in the tables, and plot the pairs of values on the coordinate plane. Use tables to compare ratios.

b. Solve unit rate problems including those involving unit pricing and constant speed. *For example, if it took 7 hours to mow 4 lawns, then at that rate, how many lawns could be mowed in 35 hours? At what rate were lawns being mowed?*

c. Find a percent of a quantity as a rate per 100 (e.g., 30 percent of a quantity means 30/100 times the quantity); solve problems involving finding the whole, given a part and the percent.

d. Use ratio reasoning to convert measurement units; manipulate and transform units appropriately when multiplying or dividing quantities.

The Number System 6.NS

Apply and extend previous understandings of multiplication and division to divide fractions by fractions.

1. Interpret and compute quotients of fractions, and solve word problems involving division of fractions by fractions, (e.g., by using visual fraction models and equations to represent the problem). *For example, create a story context for (2/3) ÷ (3/4) and use a visual fraction model to show the quotient; use the relationship between multiplication and division to explain that (2/3) ÷ (3/4) = 8/9 because 3/4 of 8/9 is 2/3. (In general, (a/b) ÷ (c/d) = ad/bc.) How much chocolate will each person get if 3 people share 1/2 lb of chocolate equally? How many 3/4-cup servings are in 2/3 of a cup of yogurt? How wide is a rectangular strip of land with length 3/4 mile and area 1/2 square mile?*

Compute fluently with multi-digit numbers and find common factors and multiples.

2. Fluently divide multi-digit numbers using the standard algorithm.

3. Fluently add, subtract, multiply, and divide multi-digit decimals using the standard algorithm for each operation.

4. Find the greatest common factor of two whole numbers less than or equal to 100 and the least common multiple of two whole numbers less than or equal to 12. Use the distributive property to express a sum of two whole numbers 1–100 with a common factor as a multiple of a sum of two whole numbers with no common factor. *For example, express 36 + 8 as 4 (9 + 2).*

Apply and extend previous understandings of numbers to the system of rational numbers.

5. Understand that positive and negative numbers are used together to describe quantities having opposite directions or values (e.g., temperature above/below zero, elevation above/below sea level, credits/debits, positive/negative electric charge); use positive and negative numbers to represent quantities in real-world contexts, explaining the meaning of zero in each situation.

6. Understand a rational number as a point on the number line. Extend number line diagrams and coordinate axes familiar from previous grades to represent points on the line and in the plane with negative number coordinates.

   a. Recognize opposite signs of numbers as indicating locations on opposite sides of zero on the number line; recognize that the opposite of the opposite of a number is the number itself, for example, $-(-3) = 3$, and that zero is its own opposite.

b. Understand signs of numbers in ordered pairs as indicating locations in quadrants of the coordinate plane; recognize that when two ordered pairs differ only by signs, the locations of the points are related by reflections across one or both axes.

c. Find and position integers and other rational numbers on a horizontal or vertical number line diagram; find and position pairs of integers and other rational numbers on a coordinate plane.

7. Understand ordering and absolute value of rational numbers.

a. Interpret statements of inequality as statements about the relative positions of two numbers on a number line diagram. *For example, interpret $-3 > -7$ as a statement that -3 is located to the right of -7 on a number line oriented from left to right.*

b. Write, interpret, and explain statements of order for rational numbers in real-world contexts. *For example, write $-3°\,C > -7°\,C$ to express the fact that $-3°\,C$ is warmer than $-7°\,C$.*

c. Understand the absolute value of a rational number as its distance from zero on the number line; interpret absolute value as magnitude for a positive or negative quantity in a real-world situation. *For example, for an account balance of -30 dollars, write $|-30| = 30$ to describe the size of the debt in dollars.*

d. Distinguish comparisons of absolute value from statements about order. *For example, recognize that an account balance less than –30 dollars represents a debt greater than 30 dollars.*

8. Solve real-world and mathematical problems by graphing points in all four quadrants of the coordinate plane. Include use of coordinates and absolute value to find distances between points with the same first coordinate or the same second coordinate.

Expressions & Equations 6.EE
Apply and extend previous understandings of arithmetic to algebraic expressions.
1. Write and evaluate numerical expressions involving whole-number exponents.
2. Write, read, and evaluate expressions in which letters stand for numbers.
   a. Write expressions that record operations with numbers and with letters standing for numbers. *For example, express the calculation "Subtract y from 5" as 5 – y.*
   b. Identify parts of an expression using mathematical terms (sum, term, product, factor, quotient, coefficient); view one or more parts of an expression as a single entity. *For example, describe the expression 2 (8 + 7) as a product of two factors; view (8 + 7) as both a single entity and a sum of two terms.*
   c. Evaluate expressions at specific values of their variables. Include expressions that arise from formulas used in real-world problems. Perform arithmetic operations, including those involving whole-number exponents, in the conventional order when there are no parentheses to specify a particular order (order of

operations). *For example, use the formulas $V = s^3$ and $A = 6s^2$ to find the volume and surface area of a cube with sides of length $s = 1/2$.*

3. Apply the properties of operations to generate equivalent expressions. *For example, apply the distributive property to the expression $3(2 + x)$ to produce the equivalent expression $6 + 3x$; apply the distributive property to the expression $24x + 18y$ to produce the equivalent expression $6(4x + 3y)$; apply properties of operations to $y + y + y$ to produce the equivalent expression $3y$.*

4. Identify when two expressions are equivalent (i.e., when the two expressions name the same number regardless of which value is substituted into them). *For example, the expressions $y + y + y$ and $3y$ are equivalent because they name the same number regardless of which number y stands for.*

Reason about and solve one-variable equations and inequalities.

5. Understand solving an equation or inequality as a process of answering a question: which values from a specified set, if any, make the equation or inequality true? Use substitution to determine whether a given number in a specified set makes an equation or inequality true.

6. Use variables to represent numbers and write expressions when solving a real-world or mathematical problem; understand that a variable can represent an unknown number, or, depending on the purpose at hand, any number in a specified set.

7. Solve real-world and mathematical problems by writing and solving equations of the form $x + p = q$ and $px = q$ for cases in which p, q and x are all nonnegative rational numbers.

8. Write an inequality of the form $x > c$ or $x < c$ to represent a constraint or condition in a real-world or mathematical problem. Recognize that inequalities of the form $x > c$ or $x < c$ have infinitely many solutions; represent solutions of such inequalities on number line diagrams.

Represent and analyze quantitative relationships between dependent and independent variables.

9. Use variables to represent two quantities in a real-world problem that change in relationship to one another; write an equation to express one quantity, thought of as the dependent variable, in terms of the other quantity, thought of as the independent variable. Analyze the relationship between the dependent and independent variables using graphs and tables, and relate these to the equation. For example, in a problem involving motion at constant speed, list and graph ordered pairs of distances and times, and write the equation $d = 65t$ to represent the relationship between distance and time.

Geometry 6.G
Solve real-world and mathematical problems involving area, surface area, and volume.

1. Find the area of right triangles, other triangles, special quadrilaterals, and polygons by composing into rectangles or decomposing into triangles and other shapes; apply these techniques in the context of solving real-world and mathematical problems.

2. Find the volume of a right rectangular prism with fractional edge lengths by packing it with unit cubes of the appropriate unit fraction edge lengths, and show that the volume is the same as would be found by multiplying the edge lengths of

the prism. Apply the formulas $V = l\,w\,h$ and $V = b\,h$ to find volumes of right rectangular prisms with fractional edge lengths in the context of solving real-world and mathematical problems.

3. Draw polygons in the coordinate plane given coordinates for the vertices; use coordinates to find the length of a side joining points with the same first coordinate or the same second coordinate. Apply these techniques in the context of solving real-world and mathematical problems.

4. Represent three-dimensional figures using nets made up of rectangles and triangles, and use the nets to find the surface area of these figures. Apply these techniques in the context of solving real-world and mathematical problems.

Statistics & Probability 6.SP
Develop understanding of statistical variability.

1. Recognize a statistical question as one that anticipates variability in the data related to the question and accounts for it in the answers. *For example, "How old am I?" is not a statistical question, but "How old are the students in my school?" is a statistical question because one anticipates variability in students' ages.*

2. Understand that a set of data collected to answer a statistical question has a distribution which can be described by its center, spread, and overall shape.

3. Recognize that a measure of center for a numerical data set summarizes all of its values with a single number, while a measure of variation describes how its values vary with a single number.

Summarize and describe distributions.

4. Display numerical data in plots on a number line, including dot plots, histograms, and box plots.
5. Summarize numerical data sets in relation to their context, such as by:
    a. Reporting the number of observations.
    b. Describing the nature of the attribute under investigation, including how it was measured and its units of measurement.
    c. Giving quantitative measures of center (median and/or mean) and variability (interquartile range and/or mean absolute deviation), as well as describing any overall pattern and any striking deviations from the overall pattern with reference to the context in which the data were gathered.
    d. Relating the choice of measures of center and variability to the shape of the data distribution and the context in which the data were gathered.

Appendix B: Sample Report Cards

REPORT CARD SAMPLE—GRADE 4

Student Name	Joshua Diggity
Grade	4
Building	Meg Tip Elementary
Principal	Mrs. Kimberly Cunningham
Marking Period	4
School Year	2020–2021

Teachers	
ELA	Mr. Anton Cardno
Mathematics	Mr. Shannon Crogan
Social Studies	Mrs. Deborah Radliff
Science	Ms. Monica Stanislas
Art	Mr. Lewis Witt
Music	Mrs. Maggie Lupo
Physical Education	Mr. Christopher Claire

Key	
Standards-based scores are based on **end-of-year expectations.** Parenthetical numbers (e.g., (2)) indicate the goal for level of understanding at that point in the year. (N/A = not applicable)	4—Exceeds expected level of understanding 3—Meets expected level of understanding 2—Meets expected level of understanding, with support 1—Shows a basic level of expected understanding, with support
Soft Skill scores identify the student's approach to learning and the learning environment. For example, a child may struggle with content but be very conscientious about the learning process. We evaluate: **Citizenship**—Effective group member, kind to peers, empathetic **Effort**—Meets deadlines, attends to details, perseveres **Attitude Toward Learning**—Strives to learn, grows from feedback	E—**Exceeds** expectations M—**Meets** expectations R—Meets expectations, with **Reminders** S—**Struggles** to meet expectations

In this report card, the English/Language Arts (ELA) and math elements are based on the Common Core State Standards, the social studies elements are based on Social Studies Practices in the New York State Social Studies Framework, and the science elements are based on the Next Generation Science Standards. All other standards are based on the New York State Standards for Learning as they exist at the time of this writing.

NOTE: The Common Core ELA Standards that connect with science and social studies are assessed as part of the Reading for Information (RI), Writing (W), and Speaking and Listening (SL) standards in ELA.

Benjabi Central School District
Home of the Bobcats!

Joshua Diggity   Grade 4   2020–2021 School Year   Meg Tip Elementary School

ELA	Marking Period	1	2	3	4
	Student can:				
RL.4. Key Ideas and Details; Craft and Structure.6	Use text-based details in works of fiction to explain or infer a text's meaning in reference to theme, character, setting, point of view, and plot.	2(2)	2(2)	3(3)	3(3)
RL.4. Craft and Structure.5	Explain major differences between poems, drama, and prose, and refer to the structural elements when writing or speaking about the text.	2(2)	2(2)	3(3)	3(3)
RL.4. Integration of Knowledge and Ideas.9	Compare and contrast similar themes, topics, and patterns of events in stories, myths, and traditional literature from different cultures.	N/A	N/A	2(3)	3(3)
RI.4. Key Ideas and Details	Use text-based details to explain or infer a text's meaning in reference to main idea and supporting details in nonfiction works.	2(2)	2(2)	3(3)	4(3)
RI.4. Craft and Structure.5 and 6	Describe the overall structure of events, ideas, concepts, or information in a text. Compare and contrast the differences between firsthand and secondhand accounts.	N/A	2(2)	3(3)	4(3)

continued

ELA	Marking Period	1	2	3	4
	Student can:				
RI.4. Integration of Knowledge and Ideas.7	Interpret information presented in a variety of forms (oral, written, maps, charts, etc.).	1(2)	2(2)	3(2)	4(3)
RI.4. Integration of Knowledge and Ideas.8 and 9	Explain how an author uses reasons and evidence to support points in a text. Integrate information from two texts on the same topic in order to write or speak about the subject knowledgeably.	N/A	2(2)	2(3)	2(3)
RL. and RI.4. Craft and Structure.4	Continue to build vocabulary through reading and to determine the meanings of words by the context in which they are used.	3(3)	3(3)	3(3)	3(3)
W.4. Text Types and Purposes.1	Write opinion pieces on topics or texts, supporting a point of view with reasons and information.	1(2)	1(3)	2(3)	2(3)
W.4. Text Types and Purposes.2	Write informative/explanatory texts to examine a topic and convey ideas and information clearly.	1(2)	1(3)	2(3)	2(3)
W.4. Text Types and Purposes.3	Write narratives to develop real or imagined experiences or events using effective technique, descriptive details, and clear event sequences.	N/A	N/A	2(3)	2(3)
W.4. Research to Build Knowledge	Conduct short research projects that build knowledge through investigation of different aspects of a topic.	N/A	3(2)	3(3)	4(3)
SL.4. Present Ideas and Knowledge.1	Engage effectively in a range of collaborative discussions with individual peers, groups, and the class.	3(2)	3(2)	4(3)	4(3)
L.4. Language	Demonstrate the use of appropriate grammar conventions in writing and speech; continue to enhance vocabulary.	2(2)	2(2)	2(3)	3(3)

Soft Skills (by quarter)	Citizenship	R	M	M	M	Effort	R	R	M	M	Attitude Toward Learning	R	R	R	R

Physical Education	Marking Period	1	2	3	4
	Student can:				
1a. Personal Health and Fitness	Participate in physical activities (games, sports) and attain a level of proficiency in three of them.	2(2)	2(3)	2(3)	2(3)
1b. Personal Health and Fitness	Demonstrate an understanding of how physical fitness leads to personal well-being; set goals to improve their personal fitness level.	N/A	2(3)	3(3)	3(3)
2a–b. A Safe and Healthy Environment	Demonstrate appropriate teamwork and sportsmanship; actively observe safety rules.	2(3)	2(3)	3(3)	3(3)
3a–c. Resource Management	Demonstrate and evaluate opportunities in their community to engage in physical activity.	N/A	N/A	N/A	3(3)

Soft Skills (by quarter)	Citizenship	R	R	M	M	Effort	R	R	R	R	Attitude Toward Learning	R	R	R	R

Art	Marking Period	1	2	3	4
	Student can:				
1b–c. Creating, Performing, Participating	Develop ideas and images based on themes, symbols, and events using the elements and principles of art (line, color, texture, shape) in order to communicate ideas.	2(2)	2(2)	3(3)	3(3)
1d. Creating, Performing, Participating	Reveal through their own artwork understanding of how art mediums and techniques influence their creative decisions.	2(2)	2(2)	2(2)	3(3)
2b. Knowing and Using Resources	Develop skills with electronic media as a means of expressing visual ideas.	N/A	N/A	3(2)	3(3)
2c–d. Knowing and Using Resources	Identify art-based professions and community opportunities for looking at original art.	N/A	3(3)	N/A	N/A

continued

Art	Marking Period	1	2	3	4
	Student can:				
3c–d. Responding/ Analyzing Works of Art	Explain the themes that are found in works of visual art, and how ideas, themes, or concepts in the visual arts are expressed in other disciplines.	N/A	2(2)	3(3)	3(3)
4a and c. Cultural Dimensions and Contributions	Demonstrate how artworks and artifacts from diverse world cultures reflect aspects of those cultures, and create artworks that reflect a particular historical period of a culture.	N/A	2(2)	3(3)	N/A
Soft Skills (by quarter)	Citizenship	R	M	M	M

Mathematics	Marking Period	1	2	3	4
	Student can:				
4.OA.A.1. Operations and Algebraic Thinking	Interpret a multiplication equation as a comparison.	3(3)	3(3)	3(3)	3(3)
4.OA.A.2 and 3. Operations and Algebraic Thinking	Use the four operations with whole numbers to solve multistep word problems.	3(3)	3(3)	3(3)	4(3)
4.NBT.A.2. Number and Operations in Base 10	Read and write multidigit whole numbers using base-10 numerals. Compare two multidigit numbers based on meanings of the digits in each place, using >, =, and < symbols.	3(3)	3(3)	3(3)	3(3)
4.NBT.A.3. Number and Operations in Base 10	Use place value understanding to round multidigit whole numbers to any place.	3(3)	3(3)	3(3)	3(3)
4.NBT.B.4. Number and Operations in Base 10	Fluently add and subtract multidigit whole numbers using the standard algorithm.	3(3)	3(3)	3(3)	4(3)

Mathematics	Marking Period	1	2	3	4
	Student can:				
4.NBT.B.5. Number and Operations in Base 10	Multiply a number of up to four digits by a one-digit number. Multiply two two-digit numbers.	3(3)	3(3)	3(3)	4(3)
4.NBT.B.6. Number and Operations in Base 10	Divide four digit numbers by a one-digit number, with remainders.	3(3)	3(3)	3(3)	4(3)
4.NF.A.1. Number and Operations— Fractions	Explain, recognize, and generate equivalent fractions.	N/A	3(3	3(3)	4(3)
4.NF.A.2. Number and Operations— Fractions	Compare two fractions with different numerators and different denominators using the symbols >, =, or <.	N/A	3(3)	3(3)	3(3)
4.NF.B.3.a,b,d. Number and Operations— Fractions	Solve word problems involving addition and subtraction of fractions referring to the same whole and having like denominators.	N/A	2(2)	3(3)	4(3)
4.NF.B.3.c. Number and Operations— Fractions	Add and subtract mixed numbers with like denominators.	N/A	3(3)	3(3)	3(3)
4.NF.B.4. Number and Operations— Fractions	Multiply a fraction by a whole number. Apply to word problems.	N/A	N/A	3(3)	3(3)
4.NF. Cluster C. Number and Operations— Fractions	Understand and compare decimal fractions (10ths and 100ths).	N/A	3(3)	3(3)	3(3)
4.MD.A.1 and 2. Measurement and Data	Use the four operations to solve problems involving measurement and conversion of measurements.	N/A	N/A	3(3)	4(3)

continued

135

Mathematics	Marking Period						1	2	3	4
	Student can:									
4.MD.A.3. Measurement and Data	Apply the area and perimeter formulas for rectangles.						N/A	N/A	N/A	3(3)
4.G. Cluster A Geometry	Draw and identify lines and angles; classify shapes by properties of their lines and angles.						N/A	N/A	N/A	3(3)
Mathematical Practices	Make use of mathematical strategies (Mathematical Practices 2, 3, 4, 5, 7, and 8).						2(2)	2(2)	3(3)	3(3)
Soft Skills (by quarter)	Citizenship	M	M	M	M	Effort	M	M	M	M	Attitude Toward Learning	M	M	M	M

Science	Marking Period	1	2	3	4
	Student can:				
4-PS3-1. Energy	Use evidence to construct an explanation relating the speed of an object to the object's energy.	2(2)	3(3)	N/A	N/A
4-PS3-2. Energy	Make observations to provide evidence that energy can be transferred from place to place by sound, light, heat, and electric currents.	2(2)	3(3)	N/A	N/A
4-PS3-3. Energy	Ask questions and predict outcomes about the changes in energy that occur when objects collide.	2(2)	3(3)	N/A	N/A
4-PS3-4. Energy	Apply scientific ideas to design, test, and refine a device that converts energy from one form to another. *(Also, 3–5-ETS1-1 and 3–5-ETS1-3)*	1(2)	2(3)	3(3)	N/A
4-PS41. Waves and Their Applications	Develop a model of waves to describe patterns in terms of amplitude and wavelength and show that waves can cause objects to move.	N/A	2(3)	3(3)	N/A

Science	Marking Period	1	2	3	4
	Student can:				
4-PS4-2. Waves and Their Applications	Develop a model to describe that light reflecting from objects and entering the eye allows for sight.	N/A	2(3)	3(3)	N/A
4-PS4-3. Waves and Their Applications	Create and compare multiple solutions that use patterns to transfer information. (Also, 3–5-ETS1-2)	N/A	2(2)	2(3)	N/A
4-LS1-1. From Molecules to Organisms	Construct an argument that plants and animals have internal and external structures that function to support survival, growth, behavior, and reproduction.	N/A	N/A	2(3)	3(3)
4-LS1-2. From Molecules to Organisms	Use a model to describe that animals receive different types of information through their senses, process the information in their brains, and respond to information in different ways.	N/A	N/A	3(3)	3(3)
4-ESS1-1. Earth's Place in the Universe	Identify evidence from patterns in rock formations and fossils in rock layers to support an explanation for changes in a landscape over time.	N/A	N/A	3(3)	3(3)
4-ESS2-1. Earth's Systems	Make observations and/or measurements to provide evidence of the effects of weathering or the rate of erosion by water, ice, wind, or vegetation.	N/A	N/A	3(3)	3(3)
4-ESS2-2. Earth's Systems	Analyze and interpret data from maps to describe patterns of Earth's features.	N/A	N/A	3(3)	3(3)
4-ESS3-1. Earth and Human Activity	Obtain and combine information to describe that energy and fuels are derived from natural resources and how their uses affect the environment.	N/A	N/A	N/A	3(3)
4-ESS3-2. Earth and Human Activity	Generate and compare multiple solutions to reduce the impacts of natural Earth processes on humans. (Also, 3–5 ETS1-2)	N/A	N/A	N/A	3(3)

Soft Skills (by quarter)	Citizenship	R	M	M	M	Effort	R	M	M	M	Attitude Toward Learning	R	R	M	M

Music	Marking Period	1	2	3	4
	Student can:				
1a. Creating, Performing, Participating	Create short musical pieces using traditional, electronic, and nontraditional sources.	3(3)	3(3)	N/A	N/A
1b. Creating, Performing, Participating	Sing songs and play instruments, maintaining tone quality, pitch, rhythm, tempo, and dynamics; perform the music expressively; harmonize.	3(3)	3(3)	3(3)	4(3)
1c–d. Creating, Performing, Participating	Read and perform simple music in ensembles.	3(3)	3(3)	3(3)	3(3)
2b. Knowing and Using Resources	Construct instruments out of nontraditional material.	N/A	N/A	3(3)	N/A
3a–e. Responding/ Analyzing Works of Art	Through listening, identify the strengths and weaknesses of specific musical works and performances, including their own and others'; describe the music's context.	3(3)	3(3)	3(3)	3(3)
4c. Cultural Dimensions and Contributions	Identify the cultural, geographical, and historical settings for the music they listen to and perform.	2(2)	2(3)	2(3)	3(3)
Soft Skills (by quarter)	Citizenship M M M M Effort M M M M Attitude Toward Learning M M M M				

Social Studies	Marking Period	1	2	3	4
	Student can:				
A. Gathering, Interpreting, and Using Evidence—1	Develop questions about New York State and its history, geography, economics, and government.	2(2)	2(2)	3(3)	3(3)

Social Studies	Marking Period	1	2	3	4
	Student can:				
A. Gathering, Interpreting, and Using Evidence—2 and 3	Analyze different forms of evidence used to make meaning in social studies, including the authorship, purpose, format, and point of view, as appropriate.	2(2)	3(3)	3(3)	3(3)
A. Gathering, Interpreting, and Using Evidence—4 and 5	Identify the arguments of, and the inferences made by, others.	2(2)	3(3)	3(3)	3(3)
A. Gathering, Interpreting, and Using Evidence—6	Create an understanding of the past by using primary and secondary resources.	N/A	2(2)	2(3)	3(3)
B. Chronological Reasoning and Causation—1, 2, and 6	Demonstrate an understanding of chronology and explain how events relate to one another along a timeline.	2(2)	3(3)	3(3)	3(3)
B. Chronological Reasoning and Causation—3, 4, 5, and 7	Recognize both short- and long-term cause and effect patterns in New York State history.	2(2)	2(2)	3(3)	3(3)
C. Comparison and Contextu-alization—1 and 4 (Also, D. Geographic Reasoning—1, 2, and 3)	Identify New York State regions geographically and recognize the relationships among geography, economics, and history.	N/A	2(2)	3(3)	3(3)
C. Comparison and Contextu-alization—2 and 3	Describe and compare historical New York State events; identify multiple perspectives for some of these events.	N/A	2(2)	3(3)	3(3)

Social Studies	Marking Period	1	2	3	4
	Student can:				
C. Comparison and Contextual-ization—5	Describe historical developments in New York State with specific detail, including time and place.	3(3)	3(3)	3(3)	3(3)
D. Geographic Reasoning—4	Recognize relationships between patterns and processes.	2(2)	2(2)	2(3)	3(3)
D. Geographic Reasoning—5	Describe how human activities alter places and regions.	N/A	N/A	3(3)	3(3)
E. Economics and Economic Systems—1, 2, and 3	Recognize the various categories of resources needed to produce goods and services, explain the impact of scarcity on decision making, and demonstrate an understanding of the role of money.	3(3)	3(3)	N/A	N/A
E. Economics and Economic Systems—4 and 5	Explain why individuals and businesses specialize and trade; explain the meaning of unemployment.	N/A	N/A	3(3)	N/A
E. Economics and Economic Systems—6	Explain the ways the government pays for the goods and services it provides, including tax revenue.	N/A	N/A	3(3)	N/A
F. Civic Participation—1 and 5	Demonstrate respect for the rights of others in discussions and classroom debates, regardless of whether one agrees with the other viewpoints; participate in negotiation and compromise.	3(3)	3(3)	4(3)	4(3)
F. Civic Participation—2, 4, and 6	Participate in activities that focus on a classroom, school, community, state, or national issue or problem, suggesting solutions as appropriate; identify where individuals can make a difference socially or politically at all levels.	N/A	N/A	4(3)	4(3)
F. Civic Participation—3	Identify different types of political systems used at various times in New York State history and, where appropriate, United States history.	2(2)	2(2)	3(3)	3(3)

Social Studies	Marking Period		1	2	3	4
	Student can:					
F. Civic Participation— 7 and 8	Identify people in positions of power and how they can influence people's rights and freedom; identify rights and responsibilities as a citizen of your community and state.		N/A	N/A	4(3)	4(3)

Soft Skills (by quarter)	Citizenship	R	R	M	M	Effort	R	M	R	M	Attitude Toward Learning	M	R	R	M

Sample Report Cards

REPORT CARD SAMPLE—GRADE 10

Student Name	Brian David
Grade	10
Building	Rosemary Gerard High
Principal	Mr. Tyrone Boggs
Marking Period	4
School Year	2020–2021
Final Average	3.7

Teachers	
ELA	Mrs. Catherine Pittman
Geometry	Mrs. Libby Keene
Social Studies	Mrs. Meg Gorton
Science	Mrs. Vicki Seybert
Art	Mr. Donald Eugene
Technology II	Mr. Ernie Alfred
Physical Education	Mr. Greg Mairs
French III	Mme. Jeanne Bisson

Key	
Standards-based scores are based on **end-of-year expectations.** Parenthetical numbers (e.g., (2)) indicate the goal for level of understanding at that point in the year. (N/A = not applicable)	4*—Exceeds expected level of understanding (= 4.1) 4—Meets expected level of understanding consistently 3—Meets expected level of understanding, with support 2—Shows basic level of understanding 1—Shows basic level of understanding, with support

Key	
Soft Skill scores identify the student's approach to learning and the learning environment. For example, a child may struggle with content but be very conscientious about the learning process. We evaluate: **Citizenship**—Effective group member, kind to peers, empathetic **Effort**—Meets deadlines, attends to details, perseveres **Attitude Toward Learning**—Strives to learn, grows from feedback	E – **Exceeds** expectations M – Usually **Meets** expectations R – Meets expectations, with **Reminders** S – **Struggles** to meet expectations
% = The percent of the final grade that the standard is worth.	Grade = The final grade for that standard (4 x %)

In this report card, the English language arts (ELA) and math elements are based on the Common Core State Standards; the social studies elements are based on Social Studies Key Ideas and Social Studies Practices in the New York State Social Studies Framework, and the science elements are based on the Next Generation Science Standards. All other standards are based on the New York State Standards for Learning as they exist at the time of this writing.

The Common Core ELA standards that connect with science, social studies, and other subjects are integrated into the listed standards.

Benjabi Central School District
Home of the Bobcats!

Brian David   **Grade 10**   **2020–2021 School Year**   **Rosemary Gerard High School**

ELA	Marking Period	1	2	3	4	%	Grade
	Student can:						
RL.9–10. Key Ideas and Details	Use text-based inferences to analyze theme and character motivations.	1(2)	2(2)	3(3)	4*(4)	10	.41
RI.9–10. Key Ideas and Details	Use text-based inferences to analyze ideas in nonfiction. Summarize objectively.	1(2)	2(2)	2(3)	4(4)	10	.4
RL and RI.9–10. Craft and Structure	Analyze how figurative language, structure, rhetoric, and point of view affect fiction and nonfiction works.	1(2)	1(2)	2(3)	4(4)	10	.4
RL.9–10. Integration of Knowledge and Ideas	Analyze the connections between a work of fiction and other works of art and writing.	N/A	N/A	2(3)	3(4)	15	.45
RI.9–10. Integration of Knowledge and Ideas	Analyze and evaluate nonfiction works in various forms of media, assessing validity, relevance, and historical value.	1(2)	2(2)	3(3)	3(4)	5	.15
W.9–10. Text Types and Purposes	Understand the elements and uses of argumentative, explanatory, and narrative texts, and can write them accordingly.	1(2)	1(3)	2(3)	3(4)	10	.2
W.9–10. Writing Skills	Produce coherent writing with strong development, organization, planning, and revision, using technology, as appropriate.	1(2)	1(3)	2(3)	3(4)	15	.3
W.9–10. Research to Build Knowledge	Effectively research, analyze, and synthesize from multiple sources to answer a question or solve a problem (both fiction and nonfiction).	N/A	2(2)	4(3)	4*(4)	10	.41
SL.9–10. Present Ideas and Knowledge	Present information effectively and as appropriate to given audiences and circumstances, using media strategically.	N/A	N/A	2(3)	4*(4)	5	.205

ELA	Marking Period		1	2	3	4	%	Grade
	Student can:							
L.9–10. Language and Vocabulary	Demonstrate the use of appropriate grammar conventions in writing and speech; continue to enhance vocabulary.		1(3)	1(3)	2(4)	3(4)	10	.3
					Final Average			3.225

Soft Skills (by quarter)	Citizenship	R	M	M	M	Effort	R	R	M	M	Attitude Toward Learning	R	R	R	R

Drawing and Painting	Marking Period		1	2	3	4	%	Grade
	Student can:							
1a–d. Creating, Performing, Participating 3c. Respond/ Analyze	Reflectively choose and effectively use various drawing and painting mediums to create a portfolio of meaningful work around a selected theme.		3(3)	4(3)	4(4)	4*(4)	50	2.05
2c. Knowing and Using Resources	Develop and execute a plan for exploring careers related to the art field, with a focus on drawing and painting.		N/A	N/A	3(3)	4(4)	10	.4
3a. Responding to and Analyzing Works of Art	Critically analyze and respond to works of art through political, cultural, social, and religious lenses, using the language of art criticism, history, and aesthetics.		3(3)	3(3)	4(4)	4*(4)	10	.41
4a and c. Cultural Dimensions and Contributions	Present a body of work within their portfolio that reflects the influences of a variety of cultural styles.		3(3)	3(3)	4(4)	4*(4)	20	.82
4a and c. Cultural Dimensions and Contributions	Interpret the meaning of artworks in terms of the cultures that produced them; explain how cultural values are both expressed in and influenced by the visual arts.		2(2)	4(3)	4*(3)	4*(4)	10	.41
					Final Average			4.09

Soft Skills (by quarter)	Citizenship	M	M	M	M	Effort	M	E	E	E	Attitude Toward Learning	R	R	E	E

Geometry	Marking Period	1	2	3	4	%	Grade
	Student can:						
G.CO.1–5. Congruence, Proof, and Construction	Experiment with transformations in the plane.	2(3)	3(4)	3(3)	4(4)	4	.16
G.CO.6–8. Congruence, Proof, and Construction	Understand congruence in terms of rigid motions.	2(3)	3(4)	3(3)	4(4)	8	.32
G.CO.9–11. Congruence, Proof, and Construction	Prove geometric theorems.	2(3)	2(4)	3(3)	3(4)	8	.24
G.CO.12–13. Congruence, Proof and Construction.	Make geometric constructions.	2(3)	2(3)	3(3)	3(4)	6	.18
G.SRT.1–3. Similarity, Proof, and Trigonometry	Understand similarity in terms of similarity transformations.	2(3)	3(3)	3(3)	4(4)	8	.32
G.SRT.4–5. Similarity, Proof, and Trigonometry	Prove theorems involving similarity.	N/A	2(3)	3(3)	3(4)	8	.24
G.SRT.6–8. Similarity, Proof, and Trigonometry	Define trigonometric ratios and solve problems involving right triangles.	N/A	2(3)	3(3)	4(4)	8	.32
G.MG.1–3. Similarity, Proof, and Trigonometry	Apply geometric concepts in modeling situations.	N/A	2(2)	3(3)	3(4)	10	.3

Geometry	Marking Period	1	2	3	4	%	Grade
	Student can:						
G.SRT.9–11. Similarity, Proof, and Trigonometry	Apply trigonometry to general triangles.	N/A	2(3	3(3)	3(4)	6	.18
G.GMD.1,3,4 G.MG.1–3 Dimensions	Explain and use volume formulas, connecting them to real-world situations.	N/A	N/A	4(4)	4(4)	3	.12
G.GPE.4–7. Algebra and Geometry	Use coordinates to prove simple geometric theorems algebraically.	N/A	N/A	3(4)	4(4)	3	.12
G.C.1–5. Circles with and without Coordinates	Understand and apply circle theorems; find arc lengths and areas of sectors of circles.	N/A	N/A	3(3)	4(4)	3	.12
G.GPE.1–2. Circles with and without Coordinates	Translate between the geometric description and the equation for a conic section.	N/A	N/A	3(3)	3(4)	3	.09
G.GPE.4. Circles with and without Coordinates	Use coordinates to prove simple geometric theorems algebraically.	N/A	N/A	3(3)	3(4)	6	.18
S.CP.1–5. Applications of Probability	Understand independence and conditional probability; use them to interpret data.	N/A	N/A	3(3)	4(4)	2	.08
S.CP.6–9. Applications of Probability	Use the rules of probability to compute probabilities of compound events in a uniform probability model.	N/A	N/A	N/A	3(4)	2	.06
S.MD.6–7. Applications of Probability	Use probability to evaluate outcomes of decisions.	N/A	N/A	N/A	3(4)	2	.06
Mathematical Practices	Make use of mathematical strategies (Mathematical Practices 2, 3, 4, 5, 7, and 8).	2(2)	3(3)	3(3)	3(4)	10	.3
				Final Average			3.39

Soft Skills (by quarter)	Citizenship	R	M	M	M	Effort	R	R	M	M	Attitude Toward Learning		S	R	M	M

Physical Education	Marking Period	1	2	3	4	%	Grade
	Student can:						
1a–b. Personal Health and Fitness	Demonstrate proficiency in complex conditioning activities; establish and maintain a high level of skilled performance; demonstrate mastery of movement forms.	2(3)	3(3)	3(4)	4(4)	30	1.2
1c, e, f. Personal Health and Fitness	Know the components of personal wellness; establish a personal profile with wellness goals; engage in activities to meet these goals; and recognize the benefits.	2(2)	2(3)	2(4)	3(4)	30	.9
2a–e. A Safe and Healthy Environment	Demonstrate responsible personal and social behavior while engaged in physical activities, with attention to safety, leadership, collaboration, and problem solving.	2(3)	4(4)	4(4)	4(4)	30	1.2
3a. Resource Management	Recognize their roles as concerned and discriminating consumers of physical activities programs and the importance of physical activity as a universal resource.	N/A	3(3)	3(3)	4(4)	10	.4
				Final Average			3.7
Soft Skills (by quarter)	Citizenship M M M M Effort M M M M			Attitude Toward Learning	M	M	M	M

Biology	Marking Period	1	2	3	4	%	Grade
	Student can:						
HS-LS1-1. Structure and Function	Construct an explanation for how the structure of DNA guides the essential functions of life through systems of specialized cells.	3(3)	4(4)	N/A	N/A	6	.24
HS-LS1-2 and 3. Structure and Function	Develop and use a model to illustrate the hierarchical organization of interacting systems that provide specific functions within multicellular organisms. Investigate and prove that feedback mechanisms maintain homeostasis.	2(2)	3(4)	N/A	N/A	6	.18
HS-LS1-6. Matter and Energy in Organisms and Ecosystems	Construct and revise an explanation that demonstrates how amino acids, other large carbon-based molecules, or both, are formed.	1(2)	3(4)	N/A	N/A	5	.15

Biology	Marking Period	1	2	3	4	%	Grade
	Student can:						
HS-LS2-3 and 4. Matter and Energy in Organisms and Ecosystems	Construct and revise an explanation for the cycling of matter and flow of energy in aerobic and anaerobic conditions; use mathematical representations to support claims as they relate to organisms in an ecosystem.	3(2)	4(4)	N/A	N/A	5	.2
HS-LS2-5. Matter and Energy in Organisms and Ecosystems	Develop a model to illustrate the role of photosynthesis and cellular respiration in the cycling of carbon among the biosphere, atmosphere, hydrosphere, and geosphere.	N/A	4(4)	N/A	N/A	6	.24
HS-LS2-1. Interdependent Relationships in Ecosystems	Use mathematical, computational representations, or both, to support explanations of factors that affect carrying capacity of ecosystems at different scales.	N/A	4(4)	4(4)	N/A	6	.24
HS-LS2-2. Interdependent Relationships in Ecosystems	Use mathematical representations to support and revise explanations about factors affecting biodiversity and populations in ecosystems of different scales.	N/A	3(4)	4(4)	N/A	6	.24
HS-LS2-6. Interdependent Relationships in Ecosystems	Evaluate claims, evidence, and reasoning as they relate to stasis and change in an ecosystem.	N/A	3(3)	4(4)	N/A	6	.24
HS-LS2-7. Interdependent Relationships in Ecosystems	Design, evaluate, and refine a solution for reducing the effect of human activities on the environment and biodiversity.	N/A	N/A	4(4)	N/A	10	.4
HS-LS2-8; HS-LS4-6. Interdependent Relationships in Ecosystems	Evaluate the role of group behavior on individual and species' chances to survive and reproduce. Create and test a solution to mitigate negative human impacts.	N/A	3(3)	4(4)	N/A	8	.32
HS-LS1-4. Inheritance and Variation	Illustrate the role of mitosis and differentiation regarding complex organisms.	N/A	N/A	2(2)	4(4)	4	.16

continued

Biology	Marking Period	1	2	3	4	%	Grade
	Student can:						
HS-LS3-1. Inheritance and Variation	Explain the role of DNA and chromosomes relating to characteristic traits.	N/A	N/A	3(3)	4(4)	4	.16
HS-LS3-2. Inheritance and Variation of Traits	Make and defend a claim that inheritable genetic variations may result from new genetic combinations, viable replication errors, environmental mutations, or all three.	N/A	N/A	3(3)	3(4)	8	.12
HS-LS3-3. Inheritance and Variation	Explain the variation and distribution of expressed traits in a population.	N/A	N/A	N/A	4(4)	4	.16
HS-LS4-2. Natural Selection/ Evolution	Construct an explanation based on evidence that supports the concept that four primary factors affect evolution.	N/A	N/A	N/A	4(4)	4	.16
HS-LS4-3. Natural Selection/ Evolution	Use statistics and probability to support the statement that organisms with an advantageous heritable trait tend to increase in proportion to those lacking this trait.	N/A	N/A	N/A	3(4)	4	.12
HS-LS4-4. Natural Selection/ Evolution	Construct an explanation for how natural selection leads to population adaptation.	N/A	N/A	N/A	4(4)	4	.16
HS-LS4-5. Natural Selection/ Evolution	Evaluate the evidence supporting claims that changes in environmental conditions may result in increases in species, the emergence of new species, extinction, or all three.	N/A	N/A	N/A	4(4)	4	.16
				Final Average		3.65	
Soft Skills (by quarter)	Citizenship	R	M	M	M	Effort	R R M M	Attitude Toward Learning	S R M M

Technology II	Marking Period	1	2	3	4	%	Grade
	Student can:						
1a-c. Engineering Design	Identify, research, and develop creative solution ideas to address a societal need, taking into consideration values, economics, ergonomics, and the environment.	3(3)	3(3)	4(3)	4*(4)	25	1.025
1d-e. Engineering Design	Design, execute, and test potential solutions, recording the results.	3(3)	3(3)	3(3)	4*(4)	25	1.025
2a-d. Tools, Resources, and Technology Processes	Investigate appropriate tools, resources, and processes that can be applied to particular projects in order to select the best fit for the team's needs.	3(3)	3(3)	3(3)	3(4)	15	.45
3d. Computer Technology	Use CADD and similar programs to model realistic solutions to design problems.	N/A	N/A	4(4)	N/A	5	.2
4b. Technological Systems	Model, explain, and analyze the performance of a feedback control system.	N/A	3(3)	3(4)	4(4)	10	.4
5a. History and Evolution of Technology 6a. Impacts of Technology	Demonstrate an understanding of how technology has affected society, and how such effects can be mitigated, planned for as society progresses, or both.	N/A	N/A	N/A	3(4)	5	.15
7a and f. Management of Technology	Use a computer-based scheduling program to plot and track the progress of a project. Demonstrate the ability to work within a team and to lead a team.	2(2)	2(3)	2(3)	3(4)	15	.45
				Final Average			3.7

Soft Skills (by quarter)	Citizenship	M	M	M	M	Effort	R	R	M	M	Attitude Toward Learning		R	M	M	M

French III	Marking Period	1	2	3	4	%	Grade
	Student can:						
1. Communication Skills— Listening and Speaking 1.a–d	Understand standard speech delivered in most authentic settings, including the main ideas and significant relevant details of extended discussions, media, or presentations. Comprehend subtler, nuanced details, including idioms.	2(2)	3(3)	4(3)	4*(4)	20	.82
1. Communication Skills— Listening and Speaking 1.e	Engage in extended discussions with native or fluent speakers on a broad range of topics that extend beyond daily lives and are of interest to the target culture.	2(2)	3(3)	3(3)	4*(4)	20	.82
1. Communication Skills—Reading and Writing 2.a–b	Comprehend the content of most texts of interest to native speakers, drawing on a broad range of learned vocabulary, idioms, and structures.	3(2)	3(3)	4(3)	4*(4)	20	.82
1. Communication Skills—Reading and Writing 2.c–d	In the target language, write multiparagraph works in which thoughts are unified and organized, using culturally appropriate vocabulary and structures.	2(2)	3(2)	3(3)	4(4)	20	.8
2. Cultural Understanding 1.a–c	Demonstrate sophisticated knowledge of cultural nuances in a target language culture, including body language and social interaction, and appropriate registers.	3(2)	3(3)	4(3)	4*(4)	10	.41
2. Cultural Understanding 1.d	Write in the target language in a manner that articulates similarities and differences in cultural behaviors.	2(2)	3(3)	4(3)	4(4)	10	.4
					Final Average		**4.07**

Soft Skills (by quarter)	Citizenship	M	M	M	M	Effort	M	E	E	E	Attitude Toward Learning	E	E	E	E

Social Studies	Marking Period	1	2	3	4	%	Grade
	Student can:						
10.1. The World in 1750	Identify, describe, and evaluate the relationships of powerful Eurasian states and empires, coastal African kingdoms, and growing European maritime empires on regional trade networks and the development of new global trade networks.	4(4)	4(4)	N/A	N/A	10	.4
10.2. Enlightenment, Revolution, and Nationalism	Describe how the intellectual shifts during the Enlightenment inspired movements that challenged political authorities in Europe and American colonial rule.	3(3)	3(4)	4(4)	4(4)	10	.4
10.3. Causes and Effects of the Industrial Revolution	Analyze the impact of Industrial Revolution innovations on population, economics, and social systems.	N/A	3(4)	3(4)	N/A	10	.3
10.4. Imperialism	Use diverse sources to identify, describe, and evaluate evidence to explore the various effects of Western European coastal interaction with Africa and Asia and the development of greater influence and connections throughout these regions.	N/A	3(3)	4(4)	4(4)	10	.4
10.5. Unresolved Global Conflict (1914–1945)	Describe, compare, and evaluate multiple historical developments (e.g., geopolitical changes, human and environmental devastation, and attempts to bring stability and peace) brought on by World War I and World War II.	N/A	N/A	4(4)	4(4)	10	.4
10.6. Unresolved Global Conflict (1945–1991: The Cold War)	Connect historical developments related to the ideological, political, economic, and military occurrences during the Cold War, and draw connections to the present.	N/A	N/A	3(4)	4(4)	10	.4
10.7. Decolonization and Nationalism (1900–2000)	Make inferences and draw conclusions from evidence about nationalist and decolonization movements, including nonviolent resistance and armed struggle, as well as the subsequent conflicts that often continued after independence.	N/A	N/A	N/A	4(4)	10	.4

continued

Social Studies	Marking Period	1	2	3	4	%	Grade
	Student can:						
10.8. Tensions Between Traditional Cultures and Modernization	Identify, compare, and evaluate multiple perspectives as they relate to historical tensions between traditional cultures and agents of modernization.	3(3)	3(3)	3(4)	4(4)	10	.4
10.9. Globalization and a Changing Global Environment (1990–Present)	Recognize and interpret the relationships between patterns and processes as they relate to the technological changes of the modern world.	N/A	N/A	3(4)	3(4)	10	.3
10.10. Human Rights Violations	Identify situations in which social actions are required, identify appropriate courses of action, and identify ways in which peopled have worked to influence those in positions of power to strive for extensions of freedom, social justice, and human rights.	4(4	4(4	4*(4)	4*(4)	10	.41
					Final Average		3.81

Soft Skills (by quarter)	Citizenship	M	M	M	M	Effort	M	M	M	M	Attitude Toward Learning	M	M	M	M

References and Resources

Black, P., & Wiliam, D. (2001, November 6). Inside the black box: Raising standards through classroom assessment. *Phi Delta Kappan, 92*(1), 81–90. doi:10.1177/003172171009200119.

Brimi, H. M. (2011). Reliability of grading high school work in English. *Practical Assessment, Research & Evaluation, 16*(17). Retrieved from http://pareonline.net/getvn.asp?v=16&n=17

Brookhart, S. M. (2013). *Grading and group work: How do I assess individual learning when students work together?* Alexandria, VA: ASCD.

Brookhart, S. M. (2017). How to use grading to improve learning. Alexandria, VA: ASCD.

Common Core State Standards Initiative. (2016a). *English language arts standards.* Retrieved from http://www.corestandards.org/ELA-Literacy/

Common Core State Standards Initiative. (2016b). *Mathematics standards.* Retrieved from http://www.corestandards.org/Math/

Cooper, H. M. (1989). *Homework.* New York: Longman.

Cooper, H. M. (2015). *The battle over homework: Common ground for administrators, teachers, and parents.* Thousand Oaks, CA: Corwin.

Council of Chief State School Officers & National Governors Association. (2010). *Common core state standards for mathematics.* Retrieved from http://www.corestandards.org/assets/CCSSI_Math%20Standards.pdf

Dueck, M. (2014). *Grading smarter, not harder: Assessment strategies that motivate kids and help them learn.* Alexandria, VA: ASCD.

Dweck, C. S. (2006). *Mindset: The new psychology of success.* New York: Random House.

EngageNY. (2015). New York state grades 9–12 social studies framework. In *New York State Common Core Curriculum*. Retrieved from https://www.engageny.org/resource/new-york-state-k-12-social-studies-framework/file/14661

Garmston, R. J., & Wellman, B. M. (1999). *The adaptive school: A sourcebook for developing collaborative groups*. Norwood, MA: Christopher-Gordon.

Guskey, T. R., & Bailey, J. M. (2010). *Developing standards-based report cards*. Thousand Oaks, CA: Corwin.

Guskey, T. R., & Jung, L. A. (2015, May). *Changing structures: Scoring and grading that reflect learning*. Lecture presented at STLE-D Workshop of Madison-Oneida Board of Cooperative Educational Services, Verona, New York.

Hargreaves, A., & Fullan, M. (2012). *Professional capital: Transforming teaching in every school*. New York: Teachers College Press.

Heath, C., & Heath, D. (2010). *Switch: How to change things when change is hard*. New York: Broadway Books.

Jensen, E. (2009). *Teaching with poverty in mind: What being poor does to kids' brains and what schools can do about it*. Alexandria, VA: ASCD.

Jung, L. A. (2009). The challenges of grading and reporting in special education: An inclusive grading model. In T. R. Guskey (Ed.), *Practical solutions for serious problems in standards-based grading* (pp. 27–40). Thousand Oaks, CA: Corwin.

Kohn, A. (1994). Grading: The issue is not how but why. *Alfie Kohn*. Retrieved from http://www.alfiekohn.org/article/grading/

Marzano, R. J. (2010). *Formative assessment & standards-based grading*. Bloomington, IN: Marzano Research Laboratory.

New York State Education Department. (2009). *Physical education learning standards*. Retrieved from http://www.p12.nysed.gov/ciai/pe/pels.html

New York State Education Department. (2011). *Standard 5–technology education*. Retrieved from http://www.p12.nysed.gov/cte/technology/standards/home.html

New York State Education Department. (2015a). *LOTE learning standards publications*. Retrieved from http://www.nysed.gov/world-languages/schools/lote-learning-standards-publications

New York State Education Department. (2015b). *The arts standards*. Retrieved from http://www.p12.nysed.gov/ciai/arts/artstand/home.html

Next Generation Science Standards: *For states, by states*. (2013). Retrieved from http://www.nextgenscience.org/

O'Connor, K. (2007). *A repair kit for grading: 15 fixes for broken grades*. Portland, OR: Educational Testing Service.

Proctor, B. D., Semega, J. L., & Kollar, M. A. (2016). Table 3. People in poverty by selected characteristics: 2014 and 2015. In *Income and Poverty in the United States: 2015*. Washington, DC: United States Census Bureau. Retrieved from United States Census Bureau website: http://www.census.gov/data/tables/2016/demo/income-poverty/p60-256.html

Reeves, D. B. (2011). *Elements of grading: A guide to effective practice*. Bloomington, IN: Solution Tree.

Sharma, R. S. (2010). *The leader who had no title: A modern fable on real success in business and in life*. New York: Free Press.

Sinek, S. (2009, September). *How great leaders inspire action*. Presented at TEDx Puget Sound. Retrieved from https://www.ted.com/talks/simon_sinek_how_great_leaders_inspire_action?language=en

Starch, D., & Elliott, E. C. (1912). Reliability of the grading of high school work in English. *The School Review, 20*(7), 442–457. doi:10.1086/435971

Starch, D., & Elliott, E. C. (1913). Reliability of grading work in mathematics. *The School Review, 21*(4), 254–259. doi:10.1086/436086

Wiliam, D. (2016). The secret of effective feedback. *Educational Leadership, 73*(7), 10–15.

Index

Note: The letter *f* following a page number denotes a figure.

About the Author

Jonathan Cornue, a former high school English teacher and integration specialist for a technical high school, is a staff and curriculum development specialist for the Madison-Oneida Board of Cooperative Educational Services (MO BOCES). He creates and presents workshops on many topics, including brain-based learning and rubric development. Jonathan coaches incoming teachers and their mentors, facilitates test development, and assists in planning changes to curricula in all grades and subject areas. As well, he writes and oversees grants, trains presenters, helps administrators refine teacher support systems, interprets state regulations for area districts, and generally lives by the mantra, "Sure, we can do that."

Jonathan, who has served on the board of the National Abolition Hall of Fame and Museum and as a member of the New York State Amistad Commission and the New York Statewide Professional Development Group, has worked with school districts across New York State and presented his thoughts on grading changes at the 2015 ASCD annual conference in Houston. A graduate of Elmira College, Jonathan earned a master's degree in education from the State University of New York at Cortland.

Jonathan can be reached at jcornue@moboces.org and you can follow him on Twitter @JonathanCornue.

Related ASCD Resources

At the time of publication, the following resources were available (ASCD stock numbers appear in parentheses):

Print Products

Educational Leadership: Lifting School Leaders (May 2017) (#117044)

Educational Leadership: Looking at Student Work (April 2016) (#116034)

Educational Leadership: Resilience & Learning (September 2013) (#114018)

Education Update: How We Got Grading Wrong, and What to Do About It (October 2013) (#113055)

How to Use Grading to Improve Learning by Susan M. Brookhart (#117074)

Grading Smarter, Not Harder: Assessment Strategies That Motivate Kids and Help Them Learn by Myron Dueck (#114003)

Transforming Classroom Grading by Robert J. Marzano (#100053)

Classroom Assessment & Grading That Work by Robert J. Marzano (#106006)

Rethinking Grading: Meaningful Assessment for Standards-Based Learning by Cathy Vatterott (#115001)

How to Create and Use Rubrics for Formative Assessment and Grading by Susan M. Brookhart (#112001)

Grading and Group Work: How Do I Assess Individual Learning When Students Work Together? by Susan M. Brookhart (#SF113073)

Charting a Course to Standards-Based Grading: What to Stop, What to Start, and Why It Matters by Tim R. Westerberg (#117010)

For up-to-date information about ASCD resources, go to www.ascd.org. You can search the complete archives of *Educational Leadership* at www.ascd.org/el.

ASCD EDge® Group

Exchange ideas and connect with other educators on the social networking site ASCD EDge at http://ascdedge.ascd.org/.

ASCD myTeachSource®

Download resources from a professional learning platform with hundreds of research-based best practices and tools for your classroom at http://myteachsource.ascd.org/.

For more information, send an e-mail to member@ascd.org; call 1-800-933-2723 or 703-578-9600; send a fax to 703-575-5400; or write to Information Services, ASCD, 1703 N. Beauregard St., Alexandria, VA 22311-1714 USA.